T0127922

Zero Days, Thousands of Nights

The Life and Times of Zero-Day Vulnerabilities and Their Exploits

Lillian Ablon, Andy Bogart

For more information on this publication, visit www.rand.org/t/RR1751

Library of Congress Cataloging-in-Publication Data is available for this publication.
ISBN: 978-0-8330-9761-3

Published by the RAND Corporation, Santa Monica, Calif.
© Copyright 2017 RAND Corporation
RAND® is a registered trademark.

Cover: Composite image by Eileen Delson La Russo.
Adapted from images by Agil_Leonardo, Matejmo, and Byakkaya; courtesy of Getty Images.

Support RAND
Make a tax-deductible charitable contribution at
www.rand.org/giving/contribute

www.rand.org

Preface

There is an ongoing policy debate over whether the U.S. government—or any government—should retain so-called zero-day software vulnerabilities or disclose them so they can be patched.[1] Those who have knowledge of a zero-day vulnerability may create "exploits"—code that takes advantage of the vulnerability—to access other parts of a system, execute their own code, act as an administrator, or perform some other action, but many worry that keeping these vulnerabilities secret can expose people who use the vulnerable software to malware attacks and other attempts to collect their private information. Furthermore, cybersecurity and the liability that might result from attacks, hacks, and data breaches using zero-day vulnerabilities have substantial implications for U.S. consumers, companies, and insurers, and for the civil justice system broadly.

The debate of whether to retain or disclose these vulnerabilities is often fueled by how much overlap there might be between the zero-day vulnerabilities or exploits the U.S. government keeps and those its adversaries are stockpiling. If both sides have the same stockpiles, then some argue that there is little point to keeping them private—whereas a smaller overlap might justify retention. But without information on the overlap, or concrete metrics based on actual data, it is challenging to make a well-informed decision about stockpiling.

To address this question, RAND obtained rare access to a dataset of information about zero-day software vulnerabilities and exploits. In this report, we explore the dataset using novel applications of traditional statistical methods to reveal a number of insights about the industry and establish some initial metrics regarding the life status, longevity, and collision rates of zero-day vulnerabilities and their exploits. We also touch on the labor time required to create an exploit. The results of this research provide findings from real-world zero-day vulnerability and exploit data that could augment conventional proxy examples and expert opinion, complement current efforts to create a framework for deciding whether to disclose or retain a cache of zero-day

---

[1] *Zero-day vulnerabilities* are vulnerabilities for which no patch or fix has been publicly released. The term *zero-day* refers to the number of days a software vendor has known about the vulnerability (Libicki, Ablon, and Webb, 2015). Zero-day vulnerabilities and their exploits are useful in cyber operations—whether by criminals, militaries, or governments—as well as in defensive (e.g., penetration testing) and academic settings.

vulnerabilities and exploits, and inform ongoing policy debates regarding stockpiling and vulnerability disclosure.

This research could be valuable to a wide variety of stakeholders, chief among them policymakers making decisions about how to reduce the nation's vulnerability while still maintaining robust options for cyber operations.

Funding for this venture was provided by philanthropic contributions from RAND supporters and from members of the RAND Institute for Civil Justice Board of Overseers and other RAND supporters, as well as income from operations.

RAND Institute for Civil Justice

The RAND Institute for Civil Justice (ICJ) is dedicated to improving the civil justice system by supplying policymakers and the public with rigorous and nonpartisan research. Its studies identify trends in litigation and inform policy choices about liability, compensation, regulation, risk management, and insurance. The institute builds on a long tradition of RAND Corporation research characterized by an interdisciplinary, empirical approach to public policy issues and rigorous standards of quality, objectivity, and independence.

ICJ research is supported by pooled grants from a range of sources, including corporations, trade and professional associations, individuals, government agencies, and private foundations. All its reports are subject to peer review and disseminated widely to policymakers, practitioners in law and business, other researchers, and the public.

The ICJ is part of RAND Justice, Infrastructure, and Environment, a division of the RAND Corporation dedicated to improving policy- and decisionmaking in a wide range of policy domains, including civil and criminal justice, infrastructure protection and homeland security, transportation and energy policy, and environmental and natural resource policy. For more information about the RAND Institute for Civil Justice, see www.rand.org/icj or contact the director at icjdirector@rand.org.

We welcome your questions and comments, which can be addressed to the lead author, Lillian Ablon (Lillian_Ablon@rand.org). For more information about the RAND Institute for Civil Justice, see www.rand.org/icj or contact the director at icjdirector@rand.org.

Contents

Figures and Tables

Figures

Tables

Summary

Zero-day vulnerabilities are software vulnerabilities for which no patch or fix has been publicly released. The term *zero-day* refers to the number of days a software vendor has known about the vulnerability (Libicki, Ablon, and Webb, 2015). Attackers use zero-day vulnerabilities to go after organizations and targets that diligently stay current on patches; those that are not diligent can be attacked via vulnerabilities for which patches exist but have not been applied. Thus, zero-day vulnerabilities and their exploits are useful in cyber operations—whether by criminals, militaries, or governments—as well as in defensive (e.g., penetration testing) and academic settings. Inevitably, a business model and markets have sprung up to trade or sell these exploitable zero-day vulnerabilities.

There is an ongoing policy debate of whether the U.S. government—or any government—should retain so-called zero-day software vulnerabilities or disclose them so they can be patched. Those who have knowledge of a zero-day vulnerability may create "exploits"—code that takes advantage of the vulnerability—to access other parts of the system, execute their own code, act as an administrator, or perform some other action, but many worry that keeping these vulnerabilities secret can expose people who use the vulnerable software to malware attacks and other attempts to collect their private information.

The debate of whether to retain or disclose these vulnerabilities is often fueled by how much overlap there might be between the zero-day vulnerabilities or exploits the U.S. government keeps and those its adversaries are stockpiling. If both sides have the same stockpiles, then some argue that there is little point to keeping them private—whereas a smaller overlap might justify retention. But without information on the overlap, or concrete metrics based on actual data, it is challenging to make a well-informed decision about stockpiling.

In an effort to address the question, RAND obtained rare access to a dataset of information about zero-day software vulnerabilities and exploits. It is a rich dataset, as some of these exploits have been found by others, but others have not. The dataset spans 14 years (2002–2016) and contains information about more than 200 zero-day exploits and the vulnerabilities they take advantage of, over half of which are publicly unknown.[1]

In this report, we explore the dataset using novel applications of traditional statistical methods to reveal a number of insights about the industry, and establish some initial metrics regarding the life status and longevity of zero-day vulnerabilities and their exploits, and the likelihood that others will discover them (known as the "collision rate"[2]). We also touch on the labor time required to create an exploit for a zero-day vulnerability. The results of this research provide findings from real-world zero-day vulnerability and exploit data that could augment conventional proxy examples and expert opinion, complement current efforts to create a framework for deciding whether to disclose or retain a cache of zero-day vulnerabilities and exploits, and inform ongoing policy debates regarding stockpiling and vulnerability disclosure.

Findings

Our research yields several interesting findings. We highlight two of these up front, and detail the others below:

1. Exploits and their underlying vulnerabilities have a rather long average life expectancy (6.9 years).
2. For a given stockpile of zero-day vulnerabilities, after a year, approximately 5.7 percent have been discovered by an outside entity.

Stockpiling may be beneficial for those offensively focused, and technically sophisticated vulnerability researchers likely prefer to stockpile vulnerabilities they find, rather than disclose them. Defenders will always be vulnerable to zero-day vulnerabilities, and likely will want to disclose and patch a vulnerability upon discovery.

Our data did not indicate that there are any vulnerabilities that are "stronger" or "weaker" than others in terms of resilience to being discovered and disclosed. It may be most efficient and cost-effective to develop an exploit for whatever vulnerability is easiest to find or whatever vulnerabilities are most effective.

Finding #1: Declaring a vulnerability as alive (publicly unknown) or dead (publicly known) may be misleading and too simplistic

Common practice is to classify a vulnerability simply as *alive* (publicly unknown) or *dead* (publicly known); however, our analysis revealed that there are several subcatego-

---

[1]   As of the time of our data cut-off (March 1, 2016).

[2]   When a two (or more) researchers independently find the same vulnerability, a "collision" is said have occurred, and the vulnerability is said to have "overlap." The collision rate is sometimes also referred to as the overlap rate.

ries of each, which can make labeling a vulnerability as either alive or dead misleading and too simplistic.

Vulnerabilities that are alive (publicly unknown) can be those that are actively sought out by defenders—these are called "living" vulnerabilities—or those that will remain in a product in perpetuity because the vendor no longer maintains the code or issues updates—these are called "immortal" vulnerabilities.

Vulnerabilities that are dead (publicly known) can be disclosed publicly by the researchers who found them ("killed by researcher") or by another party. Sometimes these vulnerabilities are disclosed with a security advisory or patch (died via "security patch"). Sometimes developers or vulnerability researchers will post a bug or vulnerability they found via a mailing list, an online blog, or a book. The poster may or may not be aware that the bug discussed is actually a security vulnerability, so there is no security advisory connected with the vulnerability (died via "publicly shared").

There are still other vulnerabilities that are quasi-alive (like a zombie), because they can be exploited in older versions but not the latest version of a product. These "code refactor" vulnerabilities get removed through revisions to the code, without being discovered or publicly disclosed as security vulnerabilities.

And because of the dynamic nature of vulnerabilities, something exploitable one day may not be the next (and vice versa).

In the course of investigating life status for our vulnerabilities, we found that Common Vulnerabilities and Exposure (CVEs) do not always provide complete and accurate information about the severity of vulnerabilities.

Finding #2: Exploits have an average life expectancy of 6.9 years after initial discovery; but roughly 25 percent of exploits will not survive for more than a year and a half, and another 25 percent will survive more than 9.5 years

After initial discovery by a vulnerability researcher, exploits have an average life expectancy of 6.9 years (specifically, 2,521 days), and any given exploit is likely to live between 5.39 and 8.84 years. Only 25 percent of vulnerabilities do not survive to 1.51 years, and only 25 percent live more than 9.5 years. The relatively long life expectancy of 6.9 years means that zero-day vulnerabilities—in particular the ones that exploits are created for gray, or government, market use—are likely old.

While our data showed that a short life is 1.5 years, this might be long enough for most vulnerability researchers.

Finding #3: No characteristics of a vulnerability indicated a long or short life; however, future analyses may want to examine Linux versus other platform types, the similarity of open and closed source code, and various groupings of exploit class type

After evaluating the vulnerability type, platform affected, source code type, and exploit class type, no characteristic statistically stood out as a "smoking gun" that might indicate a short or long life. This may have been due to either a true lack of association or a lack of statistical power to detect those associations, given the relatively small number of deaths in our dataset. More data would perhaps provide more statistically significant results, though whether that would confirm this finding or find that a particular characteristic does matter is unclear.

While nothing stood out as statistically significant, our analysis *does* provide guidance on what hypotheses may be valuable to test in future analyses—in particular, to examine the longevity of vulnerabilities for Linux compared with other platforms; to confirm the similarity of longevity of vulnerabilities for open and closed source code type; and to investigate any significance of grouping client-side and remote exploits together compared against a grouping of local, mixed, and other exploits.

Had there been characteristics that stood out (which may be confirmed or refuted with more data), that may have informed those involved with vulnerability research, the vulnerability equities process, or security in general to better refine what should be kept and what should be publicly released.

Finding #4: For a given stockpile of zero-day vulnerabilities, after a year approximately 5.7 percent have been discovered by others

The likelihood that two (or more) independent parties will discover a vulnerability in question is known as the collision rate. (When two or more researchers independently find the same vulnerability, a "collision" is said to have occurred, and the vulnerability is said to have "overlap." The collision rate is sometimes also referred to as the overlap rate.) In our analysis, collision rates changed significantly depending on the interval time used (from 40 percent to less than 1 percent), and so the timing of "flushing" a stockpile of dead vulnerabilities matters. We found a median value of 5.76 percent overlap (6.79 percent standard deviation) given a 365-day time interval, and a median value of 0.87 percent overlap (5.3 percent standard deviation) given a 90-day time interval. A 14-year interval (i.e., all of our data in one time interval) yielded a 40 percent overlap. With the exception of the 14-year interval, our data show a relatively low collision rate. This may be because those in the private exploitation space are looking for different vulnerabilities from those hunting for vulnerabilities to share as public knowledge, as well as using different techniques to find the vulnerabilities (e.g., vulnerabilities found via fuzzing, or automatic software testing, are often different than those found via manual analysis).

The data also appear to show that, in the 2002–2016 time frame, for exploits that die (i.e., are found by independent parties), death seems to happen relatively quickly and often within the first year, though the rate of discovery may not be consistent each year (e.g., vulnerabilities found post-2008 were found at a faster rate than those found pre-2008).

Our findings would be further refined with better information on how often evaluation happens (i.e., interval time used by organizations and agencies), as well as what vulnerabilities are held by other private groups.

Finding #5: Once an exploitable vulnerability has been found, time to develop a fully functioning exploit is relatively fast, with a median time of 22 days

Exploit development time ranges, but is generally relatively short. In our data, 71 percent of the exploits were developed in a month (31 days or less), almost a third (31.44 percent) were developed in a week or less, and only 10 percent took more than 90 days to exploit. The majority of exploits in our dataset took between 6 and 37 days to become fully functional (with a median of 22 days, minimum of 1 day, and maximum of 955 days).

The cost to develop (and, relatedly, the value or price of) an exploit can rely on many factors: the time to find a viable zero-day vulnerability (research time), the time to develop an exploit to take advantage of the zero-day vulnerability (exploit development time), the cost of purchasing or acquiring a device or code for review, the time to set up a test lab and the cost of the appropriate infrastructure or tools required for testing and analysis, the time to integrate a particular exploit into other ongoing operations, the salaries of the researchers involved in developing the exploit, the churn of the codebase (i.e., the likelihood of having to revisit the exploit and update it to new versions of the code to maintain a capability), and supply and demand of an exploit for a particular platform or codebase. Additional value can come from a vulnerability's uniqueness (e.g., if it is the only vulnerability found in a specific product) or the need and timeline of the customer.

Vulnerabilities purchased from external third parties had a shorter lifespan (average life of 1.4 years). This may be an argument for finding vulnerabilities and developing exploits in-house if a long life is desired.

Exploit development time does not appear to have an influence on the lifespan or survival time of an exploit.

At the most basic level, any serious attacker can likely get an affordable zero-day for almost any target. However, other tangible costs (acquiring products to find vulnerabilities in, setting up test infrastructure, renting work space, etc.) and intangible costs (premium of a high-demand, low-supply product, etc.) can cause the price to rise dramatically.

Implications for Defense and Offense

Since zero-day vulnerabilities have an average life expectancy of 6.9 years, and the overlap between what is disclosed publicly and what is found privately appears to be relatively small, offense may have an upper hand. Further, because no characteristic of a vulnerability appears to indicate a long or short life, and oversimplifying vulnerabilities as either alive (publicly unknown) or dead (publicly known) may be creating a barrier for vulnerability-detection efforts, security strategies should focus on all types of vulnerabilities, rather than just one kind.

Defenders likely need better options to both find zero-day vulnerabilities and detect when a system or software package is being exploited. In addition, rather than focusing only on finding zero-day vulnerabilities, defenders may be able to shift the balance in their favor by starting from the assumption of compromise, investigating ways to improve system architecture design to contain the impact of compromise, and adopting different techniques to identify vulnerabilities.

Those who are involved with planning offensive operations using a specific zero-day vulnerability should consider its use mostly in short-term planning circumstances. On the other hand, because there appears to be no vulnerability characteristic that indicates a shorter or longer life, it may be most efficient and cost-effective to stockpile and develop exploits for whatever vulnerabilities are easiest to find or most effective. And given vulnerabilities' long life and low collision rate, having only a few vulnerabilities as backup may be sufficient, and the use of any zero-day vulnerability for a particular software package may allow for a longer window of time to plan or carry out an operation. In addition, while potentially of limited use, vulnerabilities that are immortal or code refactored may still be valuable for operations, depending on what system or target they reside in: Researchers should consider regularly revisiting vulnerabilities they had once found to be unexploitable.

At the most basic level, any serious attacker can always get an affordable zero-day for almost any target. The majority of the cost of a zero-day exploit does not come from labor, but rather the value inherent in them and the lack of supply. Other tangible costs (acquiring products to find the vulnerabilities in, setting up test infrastructure, maintaining and porting the exploit to work on multiple versions, renting work space, etc.) and intangible costs (premium of a high-demand, low-supply product, etc.) can cause the price rise dramatically. Defenders should be aware of the availability and economics so they can defend more effectively.

To Stockpile or Not to Stockpile?

Governments may choose to keep zero-day vulnerabilities private, either for defensive purposes (e.g., penetration testing) or offensive operations. The decision to stockpile requires careful consideration of several factors, including the vulnerability itself, its use, the circumstances of its use, and other options that may be available to achieve an intended outcome.

Our analysis shows that zero-day vulnerabilities may have long average lifetimes and low collision rates. The small overlap may indicate that vulnerabilities are dense (i.e., another, different vulnerability usually exists) or very hard to find (with these two characteristics not necessarily mutually exclusive). If another vulnerability usually exists, then the level of protection consumers gain from a researcher disclosing a vulnerability may be seen as modest, and some may conclude that stockpiling zero-days may be a reasonable option. If zero-day vulnerabilities are very hard to find, then the small probability that others will find the same vulnerability may also support the argument to retain a stockpile.

On the other hand, our analysis shows that that the collision rates for zero-day vulnerabilities are nonzero. Some may argue that, if there is any probability that someone else (especially an adversary) will find the same zero-day vulnerability, then the potentially severe consequences of keeping the zero-day private and leaving a population vulnerable warrant immediate vulnerability disclosure and patch. In this line of thought, the best decision may be to stockpile only if one is confident that no one else will find the zero-day; disclose otherwise.

Acknowledgments

RAND reports typically draw on a wide collection of supporters, collaborators, and helpers in their creation. We would first like to thank philanthropic contributions from RAND supporters, income from operations, and the RAND Institute of Civil Justice for their generous support to make this research possible. Our reviewers, Allan Friedman, Director of Cybersecurity Initiatives at the National Telecommunications and Information Administration within the U.S. Department of Commerce, and Akhil Shah, senior engineer at the RAND Corporation, offered sage feedback and suggestions that greatly improved this report. RAND colleagues Martin Libicki, Cynthia Dion-Schwarz, Caolionn O'Connell, Igor Mikolic-Torreira, and Sasha Romanosky provided invaluable insights and feedback. We also thank Ernesto Amaral for his expertise and input on methodologies for evaluating demographic data, Andrea Golay for her thoughts on initial design, and David Kravitz for his statistical analysis. Christine Liu was a great resource for life expectancy methodologies. Melissa Bauman gave generously of her time to help with the flow and format, and Erica Robles was a great help with document preparation.

We sincerely appreciate those experts who took the time to share their insights and experiences, provide their input, and engage in stimulating discussions on zero-day vulnerabilities. These include Dan Geer, Katie Moussouris, Thomas Dullien, Mara Tam, Dan Guido, Wendy Nather, Steve Cristey Coley, Trey Herr, Amalie Korning Wedege, Bryson Bort, and eight exploit developers, vulnerability researchers, and brokers who asked to remain unattributed.

That we received help and insights from those acknowledged above should not be taken to imply that they concur with the views expressed in this report. We alone are responsible for the content, including any errors or oversights.

Finally, we are exceptionally grateful to BUSBY for the data.

CHAPTER ONE

Introduction

There is an ongoing policy debate of whether the U.S. government—or any government—should retain so-called zero-day software vulnerabilities or disclose them so they can be patched. Those who have knowledge of a zero-day vulnerability may create "exploits"—code that takes advantage of the vulnerability—to access other parts of the system, execute their own code, act as an administrator, or perform some other action, but many worry that keeping these vulnerabilities secret can expose people who use the vulnerable software to malware attacks and other attempts to collect their private information.

The debate of whether to retain or disclose these vulnerabilities is often fueled by how much overlap there might be between the zero-day vulnerabilities or exploits the U.S. government keeps and those its adversaries are stockpiling. If both sides have the same stockpiles, then there is little point to keeping them private—whereas a smaller overlap might justify retention. But without information on the overlap, it is challenging to make a well-informed decision about stockpiling.

In an effort to address the question, RAND obtained rare access to a rich dataset of information about zero-day software vulnerabilities and exploits. In this report, we explore the dataset, reveal a number of insights about the industry, and establish some initial metrics regarding the life status and longevity of zero-day vulnerabilities and their exploits, and the likelihood that others will discover them (known as the "collision rate"). We also touch on the labor time required to create an exploit for a zero-day vulnerability.

Little Is Known About the Extent, Use, Benefit, or Harm of Zero-Day Exploits

Software vendors aim to create flawless software, but this is aspirational. Devices, networks, systems, and processes inherently have some number of *bugs* in them; estimates range from 3 to 20 bugs per 1,000 lines of code, and one or two orders of magnitude less after thorough review (McConnell, 2004). The number of bugs varies by application, device, or method (McConnell, 2004).

A *vulnerability* is a type of bug that creates a security weakness in the design, implementation, or operation of a system or application (NRC, 1999).[1] Vulnerabilities and weaknesses can be introduced wittingly—i.e., through intentional behavior—or unwittingly, through an accidental design or implementation flaw (NRC, 2009). An *exploit* "is malicious code that takes advantage of software vulnerabilities to infect, disrupt, or take control of a computer without the user's consent and typically without their knowledge" (Microsoft, 2013). However, not all bugs are vulnerabilities, and not all vulnerabilities can be usefully exploited.[2] Some vulnerabilities may only enable an attacker to escalate privileges conduct a denial-of-service attack, while others will actually allow an attacker to gain remote code execution—often thought of as the ultimate goal—whereby the compromised system runs an attacker's code without the user's knowledge.

Zero-day vulnerabilities (or *zero-days*) are vulnerabilities for which no patch or fix has been publicly released; in some cases, the software vendor may not be aware of the vulnerability (the term *zero-day* refers to the number of days a software vendor has known about the vulnerability) (Libicki, Ablon, and Webb, 2015).[3] A *zero-day exploit* is a piece of code that takes advantage of a zero-day vulnerability and allows the exploit's creator to access other parts of the system, execute her or his own code, act as an administrator, or perform other potentially damaging deeds.[4] Zero-day exploits can be extremely valuable to those with the knowledge of them, both because every system

---

[1]   Vulnerabilities can also include misconfigurations and lack of adequate controls.

[2]   For instance, there may not always be a code path from the vulnerability to a useful part of the code. As an example, one might discover a buffer overflow, but no pathway allows exercising that buffer overflow. Or one might discover a path manipulation vulnerability, where an attacker can grab a file from a location he is not supposed to access (a common example is by inserting a command to go up to a directory to which the attacker does not have access), but the presence of a vulnerability (i.e., the attacker can move around in the file system) does not mean the implementation is available (perhaps there is a fixed/static file that is not part of any other directory, thus, nothing an attacker enters will ever get to that desired file location) (Libicki, Ablon, and Webb, 2015).

[3]   The term *zero-days* often refers to both zero-day *vulnerabilities* and zero-day *exploits*—the exploits created to take advantage of the zero-day vulnerabilities. Throughout the report, we have attempted to specify when we are talking about a vulnerability and when we are talking about an exploit.

[4]   Exploits are sometimes mistaken for implants. In this report, we focus on exploits and exploit development. There are some significant distinguishing aspects between an exploit and an implant: An *exploit* provides initial access and often the ability for code execution by taking advantage of some vulnerability in a system process, and then facilitates an implant or implant's payload, which solidifies and maintains that access (i.e., achieves persistence), and delivers some effect to the system (not just a process on the system). For example, given an actor is able to run as a user on a system, a privilege escalation exploit might modify a process to get higher-level privilege, thus allowing an implant to use a payload to then do something with that extra privilege. In other words, exploits provide access and put an actor in position to do "something." *Implants* are responsible for doing that "something." These lines sometime blur, particularly in the case of automated exploitation.

that runs the software has the vulnerability and because they can be difficult to detect and stop.[5]

Attackers use zero-days to go after organizations and targets that diligently stay current on patches; those that are not diligent can be attacked via vulnerabilities for which patches exist but have not been applied. Thus, zero-day vulnerabilities and their exploits are useful in cyber operations—whether by criminals, militaries, or governments—as well as in defensive (e.g., penetration testing) and academic settings. Inevitably, a business model and markets have sprung up to trade or sell these exploitable zero-day vulnerabilities.

While many—and perhaps most—of defensive testing or offensive operations involve known vulnerabilities (i.e., not zero-day), exploits for zero-day vulnerabilities have been used in some high-profile cases, the most famous being the Stuxnet worm, which relied on four Microsoft zero-day vulnerabilities to compromise Iran's nuclear program (Naraine, 2010). In another case, the Heartbleed vulnerability was a serious vulnerability in OpenSSL (a cryptography library used by millions of websites) that could allow private keys to be leaked and shared with an attacker. While there are no known cases of attackers exploiting Heartbleed in operations, many suspect it was used in some operations while still a zero-day.

Beyond these high-profile examples, little is known about the true extent, use, benefit, and harm of zero-day exploits. Discussions are often speculative or based on what is discovered after the vulnerability has been exploited and detected in an attack.[6] While some heuristic models have been created to examine the depletion rate of software vulnerabilities (Libicki, Ablon, and Webb, 2015), game theoretic outcomes of stockpiling (Moore, Friedman, and Procaccia, 2010), the collision rate in various code bases (Moussouris and Siegel, 2015), and the general economics of software vulnerabilities (Kuehn and Mueller, 2014), no publicly available research on this topic has been based on actual data about current zero-day vulnerabilities. In this report, we provide data-driven insights into zero-day vulnerabilities that could augment conventional proxy examples and expert opinion, complement current efforts to create a framework for deciding whether to disclose or retain a cache of zero-day vulnerabilities and exploits, and inform ongoing policy discussions surrounding zero-day vulnerabilities regarding stockpiling and vulnerability disclosure.

---

[5] Though a system with a vulnerability can avoid being exploited if there is software or hardware elsewhere in the system that prevents or mitigates the exploit's consequences.

[6] This is likely a subset of all exploits used, since presumably not all exploits operationally used are detected.

Should the U.S. Government Disclose Zero-Day Vulnerabilities?

There are policy discussions about whether the U.S. government—or any government—should retain (or stockpile) zero-day vulnerabilities for its own use or disclose them to the affected vendors for patching. When an entity stockpiles vulnerabilities and exploits for its own use, other systems that use the same software are also vulnerable (including the computers and systems of citizens, government personnel, and critical infrastructure). Some are concerned that, by stockpiling vulnerabilities and not alerting the affected vendors, adversaries or criminals will find the same vulnerabilities and use them for their own purposes.

Two factors important to this debate are

1. **Longevity of a vulnerability:** how long the vendor or public remains ignorant of the vulnerability[7]
2. **Collision rate:** the likelihood that a zero-day found by one entity will also be found independently by another.[8]

Stockpiling should not be viewed as a cut-and-dried issue ("keep them all" or "disclose them all"); there are many considerations and nuances that come into play. If an adversary finds a zero-day vulnerability, stockpiling of the same vulnerability by one's government may be harmful: Not only can the adversary can patch against anyone using it, but it may also leave a critical population vulnerable. Furthermore, who finds the zero-day makes a difference—for example, an affected vendor or a bug hunter working on the vendor's behalf, or cybercriminals or other nefarious actors who withhold the information from the vendor and the public.

On the other hand, a government's disclosure of all vulnerabilities may significantly reduce any advantage it has in using zero-days for defensive testing or offensive operations. There may be classes of vulnerabilities or certain products for which it may make sense to disclose any vulnerabilities found, and others for which it does not.[9]

---

[7] Here we are simply looking at the timeline between one entity privately finding a zero-day vulnerability and that zero-day vulnerability being publicly disclosed; we are not taking into account the time that a vendor might take to patch the vulnerability once publicly disclosed.

[8] When a two (or more) researchers independently find the same vulnerability, a "collision" is said have occurred, and the vulnerability is said to have "overlap." The collision rate is sometimes also referred to as the overlap rate.
   A *close collision* occurs where researchers find a different vulnerability in the same place in the code. See Appendix D, "Close Collisions," for more on close collisions.

[9] For example, vulnerability researchers may easily find the same buffer overflows, but each tends to find different path manipulation vulnerabilities—making a case to disclose the first class but not the second. Similarly, perhaps citizens or stakeholders of one country mostly use products of one network security manufacturer; they may want to disclose vulnerabilities found in that manufacturer's products, but not those found in a competitor's products.

There Are Many Considerations That Stakeholders Want Addressed

Government agencies, security vendors, and independent researchers have each been trying to determine which zero-days to hold on to and for how long. This generally involves understanding (1) the survival probability and expected lifetime of zero-day vulnerabilities and their exploits (longevity) and (2) the likelihood that a zero-day found by one entity will also be found independently by another (collision rate). While longevity of a vulnerability may be an obvious choice of desired metric, collision rate is also important, as the overlap might indicate what percentage of one's stockpile has been found by someone else, and possibly the types of vulnerabilities that may be more or less desirable to stockpile.[10]

To some extent, stakeholders are also interested in knowing how much it costs to find vulnerabilities and develop reliable exploits, and what their purchase price should be. Other considerations include how long a target system keeps its current configuration and version of code, how often it gets patched, how long a vulnerability should be held before it is made public, and who the target is.

There has been much discussion on this topic: Following the discovery and disclosure of the Heartbleed vulnerability in 2014, then White House Cybersecurity Coordinator Michael Daniel outlined some of the considerations.[11] Others have discussed the benefits and challenges of disclosure versus retention (Schneier, 2014), explored the various markets (Fidler, Granick, and Crenshaw, 2014; Kuehn and Mueller, 2014; Libicki, Ablon, and Webb, 2015), examined the vulnerabilities equities process (Schwartz and Knake, 2016), investigated the role of disclosure in improving or undermining security (Ransbotham and Mitre, 2011), reviewed the specific recommendations regarding software exploits from the U.S. President's Review Group (Clark et al., 2013), held industry round tables on the topic (Zetter, 2015), and opined on whether the government holding zero-day vulnerabilities weakens digital security (Crocker, 2016).

---

[10] More in-depth discussion of overlap follows later in this chapter.

[11] Former White House Cybersecurity Coordinator Michael Daniel outlined some of the considerations (Daniel, 2014):

- How much is the vulnerable system used in the core internet infrastructure, in other critical infrastructure systems, in the U.S. economy, and/or in national security systems?
- Does the vulnerability, if left unpatched, impose significant risk?
- How much harm could an adversary nation or criminal group do with knowledge of this vulnerability?
- How likely is it that we would know if someone else was exploiting it?
- How badly do we need the intelligence we think we can get from exploiting the vulnerability?
- Are there other ways we can get it?
- Could we utilize the vulnerability for a short period of time before we disclose it?
- How likely is it that someone else will discover the vulnerability?
- Can the vulnerability be patched or otherwise mitigated?

Research Questions and the Purpose of This Research

The decision to stockpile vulnerabilities likely depends on many factors independent of the vulnerabilities themselves (e.g., What kind of organization are we? How would withholding vulnerabilities harm or help us?). When the discussion moves to particular vulnerabilities, then specific questions may come into play:

1. **Life status:** Is the vulnerability really a zero-day? Is it "alive" (publicly unknown) or "dead" (known to others)?
2. **Longevity:** How long will the vulnerability remain undiscovered and undisclosed to the public?
3. **Collision rate:** What is the likelihood that others will discover and disclose the vulnerability (including other private researchers and the affected vendor)?[12]

It may be additionally helpful to know:

4. **Cost:** What is the cost to develop an exploit for the vulnerability (e.g., in order to help set purchase price)?

Answering these questions can be useful in determining which vulnerabilities to stockpile and which to patch and disclose to the vendor.[13] While there are hints that high-level criteria may exist for deciding whether to stockpile or retain vulnerabilities (e.g., Daniels, 2014), there are no publicly available metrics or hard data to inform the discussion, which makes it challenging to make a well-informed decision about stockpiling.

The purpose of this study is to establish some initial metrics regarding zero-day vulnerabilities to help inform the conversation. In particular, in this report we provide some initial metrics on the life status, longevity, and collision rate of real-world zero-day vulnerabilities and their exploits, using novel applications of traditional statistical methods—methodology that could be repeated on other sets of vulnerability and exploit data. We also touch on some of the costs and effort required to create an exploit, in terms of labor time.

---

[12] Throughout this report, we use the term *discover*. However, some might argue that *identify* or *hunt* are more appropriate (e.g., Dai Zovi, 2016). We acknowledge the differences but stick with *discover*.

[13] The decision to disclose it publicly but not to the vendor (called "full disclosure" rather than "coordinated disclosure") is based on a different set of considerations such as how mulish the vendor is or how much publicity the discoverer wants.

Intended Audience for This Research

The primary audience for this research is policymakers seeking to make the best possible decisions about how to reduce the nation's vulnerability while still maintaining robust options for cyber operations.

This research could help inform software vendors, vulnerability researchers, and policymakers by illuminating the overlap between vulnerabilities found privately and publicly, highlighting the characteristics of these vulnerabilities, and providing a behind-the-scenes look at zero-day exploit development.

This research should be of interest to those involved in the Vulnerabilities Equities Process; U.S. Department of Defense personnel who are responsible for acquisition of zero-days and developing policies regarding software vulnerabilities; the U.S. Department of Homeland Security (given its work on IDS Systems, e.g., Einstein III); the U.S. Department of State (given its role in export control topics); the military service components that are engaged with cyber effects; the FBI (which finds and prosecutes criminal activity that relies on zero-days and which uses zero-days to conduct criminal investigations); and various government offices involved in finding, creating policy around, or using zero-day exploits.

Other groups that may be interested in the research results include:

- Those who are actively looking for vulnerabilities and developing exploits for offensive purposes. The results could help them be more efficient in developing exploits for vulnerabilities that have a long life expectancy, be more frugal in developing the most time-consuming exploits (i.e., increase the benefit/cost ratio), and create representative pricing models.
- Those who are creating bug-bounty programs or buying vulnerabilities or exploits. The results could help them adjust their business models to match the efforts to find and exploit different types of vulnerabilities, and be more selective about which vulnerabilities may last the longest before detection by others.
- Those who are building software security products or are actively looking for vulnerabilities for defensive purposes. The results could provide insight into which types of vulnerabilities or classes of exploits remain undetected longest, which could be used to focus secure development efforts, or for vulnerability feeds that test new defensive measures.

Breaking Down the Zero-Day Space

Zero-day vulnerabilities and their exploits are valuable to many different communities (military and defense departments, software vendors, vulnerability researchers) and are useful both for conducting offensive operations and for strengthening defensive measures.

Different groups look for zero-day vulnerabilities: government agencies and their defense contractors, software vendors, and security researchers, either as independent contractors or employees at a vulnerability research company.

One can distinguish between those who look for zero-day vulnerabilities to exploit and keep private and those who aim for zero-day vulnerabilities to be patched and (publicly) disclosed. The composition and number of people in each group varies, as do the inventory of zero-days and funding sources.

The (Zero-Day) Vulnerability Inventory

The common understanding is that there are two types of vulnerabilities: (1) those that are retained for private use and (2) those that are part of public knowledge (see Figure 1.1). Vulnerabilities in the private space are often thought to be unpatched and used exclusively for offensive purposes. Vulnerabilities in the public space are often assumed to be known to the vendor, with a patch or fix available; once a vulnerability has made it into public knowledge, it is no longer considered a potential harm to the public.

But this view is largely oversimplified. Vulnerabilities can remain privately known but get quietly patched (so thus are no longer considered zero-day); conversely, vulnerabilities can be part of public knowledge yet still remain unpatched. Within the private knowledge space, there can be vulnerabilities that are known only to one individual or organization, and vulnerabilities that are known to multiple individuals or organizations. Some of these actors may aim to keep vulnerabilities privately known,

Figure 1.1
The Common Understanding of the Vulnerability Inventory

Private Knowledge

- Zero-day
- Vulnerabilities are unpatched
- Exploits are fully functional

Public Knowledge

- Not zero-day
- Vulnerabilities are patched and fixed
- Exploits can be proof of concept (PoC) or fully functional

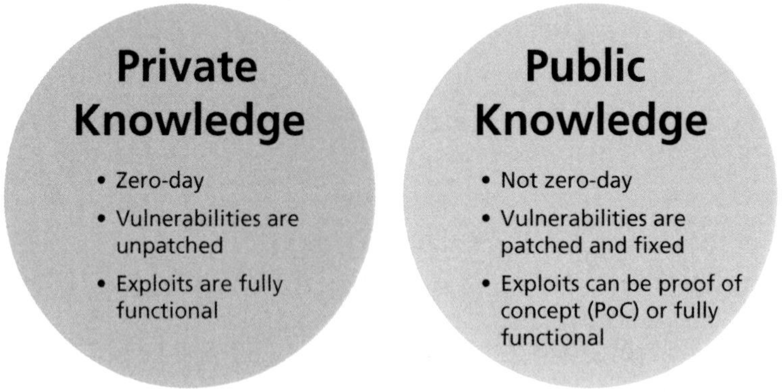

RAND RR1751-1.1

unpatched, and exploitable (i.e., zero-day), and others may aim for the opposite.[14] We thus break down vulnerabilities into the following categories:

1. Vulnerabilities that are known privately:
   a. to one individual or organization, and only that one individual or organization
   b. to more than one individual or organization (which may consider each other hostile or friendly), who both wish for the vulnerabilities to remain privately known
   c. to more than one individual or organization, one of which aims to bring the vulnerability into public knowledge space
   d. to the affected vendor (and possibly privately by others) and have been patched but are not publicly disclosed or known to be a security vulnerability.[15]
2. Vulnerabilities that are publicly known, and that may be known by the vendor and are
   a. unfixed or unpatched
   b. fixed, but only partially patched
   c. completely fixed and patched.

Over time, some vulnerabilities known only in the private space become public knowledge, for a variety of reasons (found and disclosed by an independent researcher, the affected company, a private group, etc.). Thus, over time, there will be an overlap between the private and public inventory of vulnerabilities (as shown in Figure 1.2).

Those who search for vulnerabilities and develop exploits for private use can, for the most part, be split up into two opposing groups: Blue and Red.[16] The two groups can include government agencies, defense contractors, and vulnerability researchers—consisting of independent individuals or groups of individuals and commercial exploit development shops.

Figure 1.2 shows a simplistic view and some examples of who is in each space.

Publicly disclosing zero-days that are known to both private groups but not the public—found in the purple overlap in Figure 1.2—would help Blue strengthen its defense because it would be able to protect against the zero-days that its adversaries (Red) had also found. On the other hand, publicly disclosing zero-days found in the

---

[14] Google's Project Zero would be an example of the latter.

[15] This category in particular is often overlooked in other literature on software vulnerabilities.

[16] Technically, "Red" can consist of multiple private groups; however, in this case we group them all together to represent those that might use zero-days against the interests of Blue. Furthermore, there is an assumption is that, if a vulnerability is private, it is (1) in use and (2) in use by a nation-state or criminal. But vulnerability researchers we spoke to noted that there is an under-appreciated set of vulnerabilities that just gather dust on the shelf (i.e., remain private) because they have no utility and may have properties that make the disclosure process with vendors difficult and time-consuming.

Figure 1.2
A Simplified View of Who the Vulnerability Inventory Includes

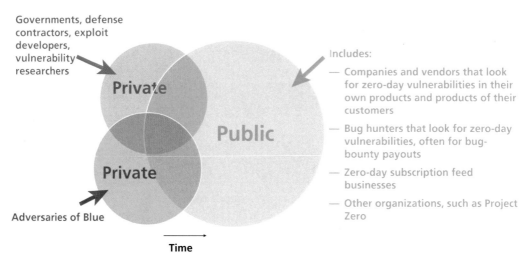

Governments, defense contractors, exploit developers, vulnerability researchers

Private

Public

Private

Adversaries of Blue

Time

Includes:

— Companies and vendors that look for zero-day vulnerabilities in their own products and products of their customers

— Bug hunters that look for zero-day vulnerabilities, often for bug-bounty payouts

— Zero-day subscription feed businesses

— Other organizations, such as Project Zero

RAND RR1751-1.2

pure blue section would hurt Blue's offensive operations and benefit Red because Red would know about the zero-days that Blue found yet still keep its own private zero-day vulnerabilities in reserve.

A big unknown is how much overlap there is between Blue and Red. Figure 1.3 shows the extremes: A great deal of overlap would support the argument for disclosing and releasing all vulnerabilities found. But if the overlap is relatively small, then the

Figure 1.3
A Simplified View of Retention Decisions

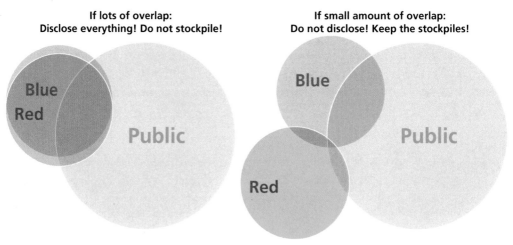

If lots of overlap:
Disclose everything! Do not stockpile!

Blue
Red
Public

If small amount of overlap:
Do not disclose! Keep the stockpiles!

Blue
Public
Red

RAND RR1751-1.3

two groups are finding different vulnerabilities, and disclosing what Blue has might leave Blue in a weaker state. In that case, retention may be valuable.[17]

Data for This Research

RAND obtained a dataset of information about zero-day software exploits through a research connection.[18] It is a rich dataset, as some of these exploits have been found by others and some have not. The dataset spans 14 years (2002–2016) and contains information about more than 200 zero-day exploits and the vulnerabilities that they take advantage of, over half of which are unknown to the public.[19] The data we received had a final count of 207 exploits, after approximately 20–30 were removed due to operational sensitivity.[20]

The data cover many aspects of an exploit and the software vulnerability it takes advantage of: types of products, vendors, source types, vulnerability types, and exploit types. It also includes dates specifying when a vulnerability was first determined to be worthwhile to develop into a fully functioning exploit, when an exploit had been created, and if and when the vulnerability was found externally by a third party. It also contains information on the analyst who wrote the exploit and the relevant security bulletin (where applicable).

The dataset contained numerous categories per entry, and there are a myriad of things that one could study about it. In this report, we perform some first-order analysis to determine a variety of metrics related to zero-day vulnerability life status, survival rates, collision rates, and costs (determined by time to develop exploits). More details on the data can be found in Appendix G, "More Information About the Data."

The data came from a vulnerability research group (which we will call BUSBY to protect its anonymity).[21] Some BUSBY researchers have worked for nation-states (so their skill level and methodology rival that of nation-state teams), and many of BUSBY's products are used by nation-states. Thus, these data are a proxy for what Blue—or a sophisticated private use group—has, and can be used to explore a variety of questions related to zero-day vulnerabilities, including the longevity and lifetime of zero-day vul-

---

[17] As was previously mentioned, this decision calculus is not simple.

[18] The source of the data has deep experience participating in both the private use (gray) and public knowledge (white) markets.

[19] As of our information cut-off date of March 1, 2016.

[20] The exact number is unknown.

[21] A busby is a type of military hat that reached popularity in early 20th century. We find it a fitting cover term because (1) it is playful reference to the many types of hats (white, gray, black) of vulnerability researchers and (2) zero-day exploits are most often used by military components.

nerabilities, the types of vulnerabilities that last the longest before detection by others, and the types of products that contain exploitable zero-day vulnerabilities.

Ideally, we would want similar data on Red (i.e., adversaries of Blue, or other private-use groups), to examine the overlap between Blue and Red, but we could not obtain that data. Instead, we focus on the overlap between Blue and the public (i.e., the teal section in the figures above) to infer what might be a baseline for what Red has. We do this based on the assumption that what happens in the public groups is somewhat similar to what happens in other groups. We acknowledge that this is a weak assumption, given that the composition, focus, motivation, and sophistication of the public and private groups can be fairly different, but these are the only data available at this time.

With our data, we know the size of the overlap between private use vulnerabilities and public knowledge vulnerabilities (i.e., the teal overlap between the blue and green in Figure 1.4).

Our research focuses on the characteristics of vulnerabilities that are in the overlap between Blue (or a reasonable proxy for Blue) and the public (i.e., the blue and teal sections). We sought to understand the size of the overlap and the lifetime or longevity of zero-days held privately before they are discovered publicly. We use this to create a floor for overlap and lifetime of zero-day vulnerabilities. This lower bound would provide an indicator and help inform the discussion of stockpiling. Further insights into the inventory of some of Blue's most sophisticated adversaries (or other groups that find zero-days for private use) would lead to a more refined estimate of overlap and lifetime.

While our intent was to perform analysis and derive results from the data and quantitative measures, we also sought out the qualitative expertise from others in the vulnerability research community. In addition to in-depth conversations with those

Figure 1.4
Our Data

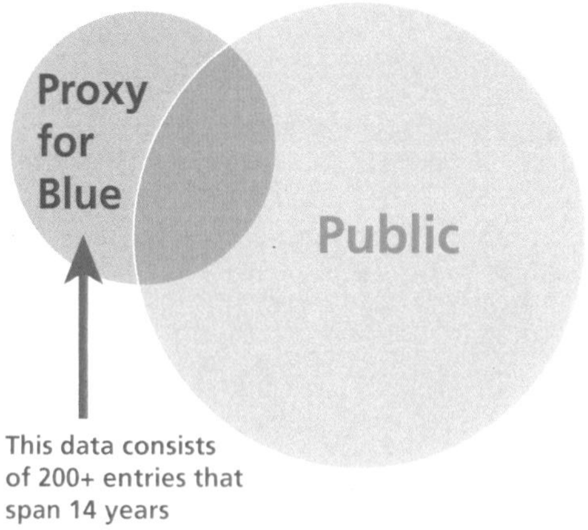

Proxy for Blue

Public

This data consists of 200+ entries that span 14 years

RAND RR1751-1.4

who provided the data, we spoke with vulnerability researchers from three gray-market companies (i.e., researchers who write exploits for government or private-use customers), those at two large commercial companies that have their own in-house vulnerability research team, those at companies that run bug-bounty programs, and other experts who have published on this topic or who have had other experience with the buying, selling, brokering, or developing of zero-day vulnerabilities.

Methodology of Research and Data Collection

Our Data Contain Characteristics About Each Exploit
Our dataset was created by culling relevant information from the exploit code itself. We collected information about various characteristics of each exploit:

- vulnerability type (at a high and low level)
- platform type (high and low level)
- exploit class
- source code type
- vendor.

More information and a breakdown of frequencies is provided in Appendix G, "More Information About the Data."

Collecting the Data and Determining Lifetime Dates
Three analysts spent a week systematically working through repositories of exploit code and detailed exploit documentation of more than 200 exploits, pulling out information about the vulnerability exploited, platform affected, life status, lifetime, and other relevant information.

The three dates possible for each exploit are as follows:

1. **Birth date:** The date a vulnerability was discovered and determined to be worth creating a fully functioning exploit for.[22] This date was most often obtained from the repository log check-in. When the repository logs were not available, we used the dates on the exploit documentation when the exploit developer kept

---

[22] Only a subset of zero-day vulnerabilities are exploitable, so when exploit developers find vulnerabilities, they must determine whether or not they are able to develop an exploit. Many factors can come into play when deciding whether an exploit will be developed to take advantage of the vulnerability. For example, there may be other vulnerabilities or bugs standing in the way of exploiting the intended vulnerability (see discussion of "blocker bugs" later in the report), the vulnerability may not lead to anything useful (yet), or the exploit developer may already have several exploits in the same place in code on the shelf, so they will use their time on other vulnerabilities (for example, in this dataset, 14 percent of the entries only made it to the "proof of concept" stage and fully functioning exploits were not created).

a timeline of her or his work. In the cases when these dates were not available, we used the creation date of the document (i.e., when the exploit developer first started writing about the vulnerability found). In a few cases, we relied on the recall of the exploit developer who had been involved with the specific exploit. In some cases, when an initial discovery date was not available, the birth date was the date that a cursory proof of concept (PoC) exploit had been developed.[23]

2. **Mature date:** The date of the first fully functioning, reliable exploit (i.e., the exploit was ready to be delivered to a client or used in operations).[24] This date was obtained from the exploit documentation and repository logs.[25]

3. **Death date** (if applicable): The date when the vulnerability was discovered and disclosed to the public by an outside third party; this is only applicable to some of the vulnerabilities and exploit in our dataset.[26] We used search engines to perform online searches of strings, libraries, functions, variables, and other unique identifying information that was specific to the vulnerability, was the basis of the exploit, or was instrumental in achieving exploitation. In addition to using basic search engine methods, we examined various repositories where known vulnerabilities are reported (e.g., Common Vulnerabilities and Exposures [CVE]/National Vulnerability Database [NVD], Open Sourced Vulnerability Database [OSVDB], Bugtraq, SecurityFocus).[27] The three analysts each spent approximately 30–45 minutes per vulnerability to search. In the cases in which no results appeared, we searched for *any* reported vulnerability on the product and analyzed those results to see whether our particular vulnerability

---

[23] That is, code that demonstrates or proves that a vulnerability is exploitable. For more detail on proof-of-concept exploits, see Chapter Two and Appendix A, "The Exploit Development Cycle."

[24] There were some cases in which follow-on work needed to be done to make the exploit reliable for multiple versions, but this timeline was not captured.

[25] These dates are fairly accurate, as exploit developers tend to be quite excited, proud, and eager to share with their colleagues when one of their exploits is fully functional and reliable.

[26] Another way to determine whether a vulnerability was still a zero-day and its exploit was still viable would be to try the exploit on the latest version of the product. We did this in a few cases; however, in most cases we were not given approval to test the exploit to see whether it was still alive. Therefore, we have relied on the methodology noted here to determine whether a vulnerability was still zero-day or not.

[27] We acknowledge that not all publicly known vulnerabilities are encompassed by these repositories. Some experts in the vulnerability disclosure space we spoke with estimated that vulnerabilities listed in the OSVDB (now called VulnDB) represent approximately 80 to 90 percent of all known vulnerabilities (including all vulnerabilities listed in CVE/NVD), and vulnerabilities listed in CVE/NVD represent approximately 50 percent of those vulnerabilities in OSVDB/VulnDB. Vulnerabilities not in OSVDB (and thus, not in CVE/NVD) were thought to be largely bugs found in live websites—often the focus of bug-bounty programs. They noted that, for those vulnerabilities in OSVDB/VulnDB but not in CVE/NVD, there was a high likelihood that a patch did not exist and that vulnerability scanners had not yet found them. These vulnerabilities were thought to be in industrial control, automotive, and medical systems.

matched or could be reasonably assumed to match.[28] Sometimes, discovering that a vulnerability had been discovered meant scouring listservs.[29] In a few instances, people had described the vulnerability in a listserv as simply an error (rather than a security vulnerability), and there was no indication that a security bulletin or public advisory of the vulnerability had been made. We still considered these vulnerabilities dead, since the information was made public—regardless of whether it was specifically mentioned as a security issue. In a very few cases, the exploit developers whom the authors worked with had a "gut feeling" that a vulnerability was detected, but we could not find proof.[30] In these cases, we marked the exploit as "uncertain."

To determine dates, we used the timestamps on the repository logs. Because some of the exploits were older and the documentation was done by the actual exploit developer, some documentation was more thorough than others. While the details of the exploit were always thorough, obtaining exact dates was not always achievable. As a result, we lack information about birth date and maturity date or only have a month and year associated with a subset of the 207 exploits.[31] This affected our sample size for analysis, as it meant that we could use only those with complete information for performing survival analysis and calculation of expected lifespan. In the cases where we had only the month and year timestamp for the birth date, we defaulted to the first of the month, so, in some cases, there may be up to a 30-day range. But because this was only for the birth date, and not the mature date, the numbers may be conservative for time to develop an exploit. In a few cases, we relied on the personal recall of those who had been directly involved in the exploit development for how long it took to exploit.[32]

We used birth and death dates for our calculations of longevity and collision rates, as those indicate dates of first discovery by private researchers (birth) and first disclosure to the public (death). The mature date is important in calculating the time it takes to develop a fully functional exploit.

---

[28] This brought some interesting findings to light. For example, a CVE entry that publicly listed a vulnerability as causing a denial of service was privately used by BUSBY to provide privilege escalation (something often considered more severe and sophisticated than a denial of service).

[29] Some have argued that discussion of a vulnerability on publicly available listserv does not warrant that vulnerability being considered "known," "dead," or no longer a zero-day. We acknowledge that it is acceptable to consider those vulnerabilities alive and zero-day—but for the purposes of our research, we count them as dead.

[30] To definitively determine whether the vulnerability existed, we would have needed to download the applicable version of source code and search for the vulnerability.

[31] Only 61 percent of our data had the criteria we needed for these calculations.

[32] We acknowledge that humans tend to be inaccurate with respect to recall. That said, those that were performing the recall did so for only a small number of our sample, and were experts in the topic, so perhaps had more accurate recall.

Organization of This Report

The rest of the report is organized as follows. Chapter Two provides more background and depth into the nature of zero-day vulnerabilities, the exploit development process, business models, and the security researchers themselves. Those already familiar with this topic may wish to skip directly to Chapter Three, where we dive into analysis of the data and discuss the different life stages for an exploit; survival probability and life expectancy estimates; collision rate; and an initial look at the cost to develop an exploit. Chapter Four concludes with implications and recommendations. Our appendixes contain additional information about the exploit development cycle (Appendix A) and the vulnerability researchers (Appendix B), a case study on how mitigations have affected exploitability (Appendix C), an investigation of close collisions (Appendix D), a first order look at cost and pricing considerations for zero-day exploits (Appendix E), and additional charts (Appendix F) and information about the data (Appendix G) that may be of interest to the reader. Appendix H provides a glossary of terms and definitions to supplement the reader's understanding of software vulnerabilities and exploits.

CHAPTER TWO

More Discussion of Zero-Day Vulnerabilities

Chapter One provided a brief background on zero-day vulnerabilities. This chapter provides more detail about the complex nature of zero-day vulnerabilities, the exploit development process, business models, and security researchers. When possible, we provide concrete examples from our data and discussions; we also provide more information in the appendixes.

Nature of Zero-Day Vulnerabilities

Vulnerabilities Are Dynamic

Vulnerabilities are dynamic: the usefulness of an error may differ depending on where it is in code.[1] Furthermore, not all errors are vulnerabilities, and not all vulnerabilities can be usefully exploited. The usefulness of an error in code can change from one day to the next: A vulnerability that is not initially exploitable may eventually be exploitable in future code bases (and vice versa).[2] New access methods and techniques are constantly being developed that allow the use of previously unexploitable vulnerabilities, and mitigations are similarly introduced that prevent the further use of currently exploitable vulnerabilities.[3] In one case, BUSBY researchers discovered a design flaw vulnerability that allowed for the remote code execution of arbitrary binaries in a specific location, which most consider a high-impact vulnerability, but it needed to be

---

[1] For example, a null dereference error in *user space* is generally considered difficult to exploit; a null dereference error in the *kernel* has historically been easier to exploit. A null dereference vulnerability is one where a memory address is zeroed out or set to zero before it gets its first reference. In user space, one must work with dynamic allocations, different compiled versions, etc., but in the kernel, generally just one compiled distribution exists.

[2] For example, a vulnerability can achieve newfound exploitability due to changes in the code or compiler that remove a "blocker bug"—bugs that do not lead to anything useful but will cause a crash or get in the way of some other bug that can be exploited. Some exploit developers have contemplated submitting those blocker bugs to the affected vendor to be fixed so they can get to the exploitable bugs. In other words, in lieu of the exploit developer being able to introduce a vulnerability into the source code (because they are not part of the vendor core development team), the "blocker bug" submitted for patch allows the introduction.

[3] For example, the introduction of call flow graphing in Windows 10.

combined with other vulnerabilities to enable write access to that location to achieve any effect (i.e., if one cannot write the code to be executed, simply having the execute ability is not as valuable). Waiting for a high-impact bug to become an exploitable vulnerability can be frustrating: The means for it to be exploitable may never emerge, or the vulnerability may be discovered and patched before it is usable.[4] That said, while it can be time-consuming to check for exploitability after every new code release, many exploit developers see it as more cost-effective to keep track of vulnerabilities that they have already found but that may not currently be exploitable, rather than trying to find new vulnerabilities, which is generally seen as more resource-intensive than exploitation.[5] Because a vulnerability's severity or impact can vary depending on the location in code, reliance on other vulnerabilities, or goal of the operator using an exploit, placing a static score may be misleading.[6]

Exploit Development Basics and Considerations

Developing a reliable exploit is challenging; operational considerations (including the operator and mitigations) can lead to uncertainties and decreased reliability. Ideally, an exploit will work on every configuration and version of a target, but the only true test is running the exploit on the intended target. Because testing in an operational setting is not generally feasible, vulnerability researchers take different approaches to reduce uncertainty and increase reliability in operational settings. Some create spreadsheets that matrix various versions and configurations tested against, and test each arrangement 1,000 or so times. Others examine the exploit—and the operational setting of the target, to the extent possible—and attempt to find the remaining unknowns and chances for failure. This means making sure that the primitives (the building blocks of an exploit) are as reliable as possible, which may depend heavily on the type of vulner-

---

[4]   For example, a null dereference vulnerability found by researchers in user space was determined not to be accessible; the researchers waited until a new code version revealed a vulnerability in the kernel, providing a way to access the user space vulnerability and create a useful exploit. In another case, researchers told us of a vulnerability in a commonly used wireless application that would have required too much effort to exploit (e.g., it might require special hardware to access). Thus, the analysts set it aside and return to it every so often to check whether some new vulnerability has emerged that would assist in exploitation.

[5]   For the cases in our data where no exploit was created (although exploitable vulnerabilities were found), approximately half were not exploited because certain capabilities were required or conditions needed to be true; the others were not exploited because the analysts already had plenty of coverage in the particular codebase.

[6]   That said, impact ratings, such as those from the Common Vulnerability Scoring System (CVSS), can be useful from a defensive posture, and are understood to be applicable in the specific time and context the vulnerability was found. On the other hand, impact and severity ratings may not always be accurate: For example, BUSBY researchers found and exploited a vulnerability that was a highly impactful memory mismanagement vulnerability (allowing an out-of-bounds write), but was reported in the CVE as medium criticality as a denial-of-service bug.

ability being exploited.[7] And because an exploit can consist of several vulnerabilities chained together, a normally reliable vulnerability can be combined with an iffy vulnerability to create an unreliable exploit, or an exploit that reliably works on a physical system may behave drastically differently on a virtual machine.[8]

Researchers may also try to determine the baseline information about a target, such as system load and configuration; network lag, fragmentation, and architecture; and memory usage, architecture, and availability. Countermeasures and mitigations, such as load balancers and detection mechanisms, auto-update prevention, patch existence (whether or not applied), and intrusion and prevention systems, also factor in. It can help if the exploit developer knows the nature of the intended follow-on implant.[9] Uncertainty about the reliability of an exploit can also depend on the skills of the operator who is employing the exploit and how well the operator knows the target environment.[10] Whatever the approach, testing is still done in a lab setting, with little of the variance from debug settings, language packs, latency, and bandwidth that can affect the success and reliability of an exploit in an operational setting.

An exploit may be a "single-shot" exploit that allows for a single attempt at exploitations (e.g., a single stack overflow in a process that will become unavailable if the exploit fails), or it may need to exploit many things in sequence or repeat the exploitation attempt multiple times.[11] Once the vulnerability researcher sells or leases an

---

[7] For example, vulnerabilities that exist in certain places in code (e.g., user space), or are of certain types (e.g., command injection, SQLi, stack overflow) are generally reliable. But vulnerabilities that lead to a heap overflow or require timing or race conditions may not be as reliable.

[8] Here we are talking about reliability for exploits, not implants or "payloads." Reliability is desired for exploits, but it is not always guaranteed. Reliability for an implant, however, is critical. While an exploit provides initial access, an implant maintains that access, persists, and delivers some effect. If an implant is unreliable, it could lead to blue-screening a box and damaging a sensitive operations. Implants are very hard to maintain, so they command a hefty price. One estimate is $1 million per implant.

[9] For example, if the customer plans to use a payload for data egress, then the exploit developers need to be aware of the exfiltration route and what countermeasures (e.g., firewalls), if any, are in place.

[10] Operational use is up to the customer; the exploit developer can only provide feedback and hope that the operators will know what to do. If an exploit is not performing in an operational setting as it did in the lab environment, the operator may need to determine characteristics of her target environment that are affecting the exploit (e.g., using the exploit during times of high traffic—and thus high latency and congested bandwidth—on a target system; a savvy operator may recognize the need to wait until off-hours to use the exploit). Some operators are better at this than others.

[11] Sometimes, multiple exploits can be used in different phases to reduce uncertainty and increase reliability. For example, information leak vulnerabilities can be used in initial phases for reconnaissance and fingerprinting, to aid development for follow-on exploits. If the payload used by the operator after initial exploitation requires egress, then there may be requirements to know about the route of exfiltration (e.g., what firewalls or countermeasures may be in place, or what protocol the payload needs to be wrapped in). Another part of the exploit may be in charge of cleaning up the presence of an exploit by removing logs, ensuring continuation (i.e., no crashes) and persistence, exiting threads, and rewinding the state of the target system.

exploit to a customer, the transaction is complete; it is up to the customer how and whether to use the exploit.

Exploit Development Cycle

The exploit development process consists of many steps, and each step can go through multiple iterations. The first stage of exploit development is to create a proof of concept (PoC), generally to prove that code execution can be achieved for one case or version. A fully functional exploit expands a PoC to be useful for every possible version of a system.[12] Exploits often also come with documentation for an operator (including information about system latency, bandwidth requirements, and possible secondary effects, such as log entries left behind and what needs to be cleaned up). For more details about the exploit development cycle and some factors that go into exploit development, see Appendix A, "The Exploit Development Cycle."

People in the Zero-Day Vulnerability Space

Some vulnerability researchers focus on finding zero-day vulnerabilities and giving them to the affected vendor, sometimes for a fee and sometimes for recognition.[13] Often, these vulnerabilities go into the public domain through advisories and published vulnerability notices.[14] This group of "white hat" bug hunters is growing, due to the increasing popularity of bug-bounty programs from companies, like HackerOne and BugCrowd. Many software vendors have their own internal groups tasked with finding zero-day vulnerabilities in the company's software and any software the company uses.[15] Companies such as Exodus Intelligence, ZDI, and iDefense provide a "zero-day feed" that their subscribers can use for defensive testing and for implementing protective measures in products. The vulnerabilities generally make it back to the affected vendor. The goal is often 90 days, though that timeline can vary.[16] The researchers who participate in bug-bounty programs or who sell to feeds generally focus on finding a

---

[12] This is when the exploit gets additional logic: for example, a memory or information leak, brute force algorithm, or potentially a list of addresses to try on different versions.

[13] This group is in the right-hand side of Figure 1.1.

[14] There are various publicly available databases containing information about discovered vulnerabilities (that may or may not be patched). Some popular ones have been the NVD and the freely available ODSVDB, which is now the payment-required VulnDB (Risk-Based Security, 2017).

[15] For example, Cisco's Talos group.

[16] Upon discovering some zero-day vulnerabilities that had remained undetected for four years, Exodus Intelligence changed its policy of never disclosing a vulnerability found to instead disclosing 90 days after notifying the vendor (Exodus Intelligence, 2016).

vulnerability and developing a basic PoC exploit for it. Researchers within Google's Project Zero also aim to find vulnerabilities and provide their findings to the vendor within 90 days, but they go beyond a PoC to create a fully functional exploit in order to determine the true impact. As such, they are similar to researchers who seek out vulnerabilities for private use.

Vulnerabilities that remain privately held are sometimes patched quietly or simply held unpatched.[17] The group that seeks zero-day vulnerabilities for private use generally consists of researchers who look for vulnerabilities to be used for operational purposes—both offensively and defensively—and can consist of "gray hat" nation-state actors or defense contractors (of any country), "black hat" cybercriminals, or hobbyists with various motives.[18] The most sophisticated aim to not only find zero-day vulnerabilities but also to create fully functional exploits for them.

While exact numbers are unknown, many estimate that the number of people in the "public" group is at least an order of magnitude larger than the number of people who search for zero-days and create exploits for private use. There are essentially three tiers of vulnerability researchers.

Those in the top tier are very skilled and range from a single contractor working alone, to a team of a dozen, to a company in the (low) hundreds. Exploits written by members of this tier are high-quality and reliable. A majority of those in this tier are in the gray markets—finding exploits for private use or for sale to governments or defense contractors—although white-market researchers who find vulnerabilities to share as part of public knowledge also exist, and there can be fluidity between gray and white hats depending on the funding and resources available (e.g., many researchers at Google's Project Zero came from government or gray-market teams). The number of researchers at this top level is thought to range between 300 and 3,000.[19] Many believe that it is becoming harder to author a reliable exploit because vendors are getting better at patching and because mitigations aim to cover wide classes of vulnerabilities.

Those in the intermediate tier have the ability to find vulnerabilities and write exploits that work against low-hanging vulnerabilities and targets, but they may not be capable of writing exploits against hard targets and may rely on off-the-shelf tools or retooling existing exploit code for their own use. Some believe this intermediate class drives the cybercrime markets.

---

[17] This group is in the left-hand side of Figure 1.1.

[18] For example, a hacker named "Phineas Fisher" found and used a zero-day vulnerability to penetrate the systems of the gray market group Hacking Team to exfiltrate data and source code (Zorabedian, 2016).

[19] One expert estimated that 300 researchers serve the United States and likely 1,500 exist worldwide. Others estimated a maximum of 1,000–2,000 researchers worldwide. Another person familiar with the space estimated 3,000 researchers work for U.S. defense contractors and similar numbers work for other countries. For example, Chinese company Tencent's Keen Security Lab is thought to have about 3,000 security researchers, though not all are thought to have the highest skills and abilities.

At the bottom are the bug hunters who do not go beyond finding vulnerabilities and perhaps showing a hypothetical exploitation. The skill required at this level can be taught. Most agree that the number of researchers in the lowest tier is at least an order of magnitude larger than in the highest tier. For example, there are more than 26,000 researchers on the BugCrowd platform (though it is unclear how many are active bug hunters, as only ten have collectively made 23 percent of the total payouts), a few thousand reportedly signed up to hunt for bugs on HackerOne, and almost 8,000 have contributed to Wooyun's vulnerability disclosure program.[20] The types of vulnerabilities found by each tier are thought to be relatively distinct, though some overlap can occur. More discussion on the characteristics, career length, and seasonality of exploit developers is in Appendix B, "The Vulnerability Researchers: Who Looks for Vulnerabilities?"

Business Models

Markets for Zero-Day Vulnerabilities

Markets for zero-day vulnerabilities have been growing in recent years and are distinguished by who the initial buyer is, the public versus private nature of the vulnerability, and the intended use of the vulnerability.[21] Those in the white market seek to immediately turn their vulnerabilities over to the affected vendor (often moving them into the public knowledge space) and use them for defensive purposes. In the gray market (also sometimes called the government market), vulnerabilities remain private, are used for either offensive or defensive purposes, and may eventually be disclosed to the affected vendor, though that is not guaranteed because they are typically first sold to a government, military, or defense contractor.[22] Black markets sell zero-day vulnerabilities for criminal use or illicit purposes and aim to keep the vulnerabilities private.

Those who develop and then sell or lease fully functioning exploits garner more money than those who just find vulnerabilities or create a PoC, because purchasers of the former are buying the guarantee that the exploit is reliable, effective, and, in some

---

[20]   More than half of the researchers that signed up on BugCrowd's site are from India and the United States (BugCrowd, 2016; Zhao, Grossklags, and Liu, 2015).

[21]   Another way to differentiate between markets can be by timeline: In the white market, a vulnerability is often given to the vendor without delay. In the gray market, a vulnerability may make it back to the vendor but after a delay or use by someone else. In the black market, a vulnerability generally never makes it back to the vendor.

[22]   Some in the gray market believe they are part of the white market because they operate within the law, and thus are deserving of the "white" coloring. However, we distinguish by the initial recipient of the vulnerability or exploit derived from the vulnerability, not whether the market participant is acting within or outside the law. Because the gray-market customer tends to be part of or associated with the government, another term for the gray market could be the government market.

cases, able to avoid detection. As such, PoC exploits are generally an end goal for white hat researchers, whereas the gray and black markets deal in fully functioning exploits.[23]

Buyers and sellers have shifted over time. In years past, the use of third parties, brokers, and "cutouts" were common to move exploits, but that is not generally the case today: Given a long enough relationship, or the right connections, exploit development organizations prefer to work directly with a customer, because doing so allows for more control over what happens to the exploit. One vulnerability research team we spoke with noted that they had bad experiences with brokers reselling exploits to multiple parties and, in another case, the broker sharing the exploit with the broker's own partners. Additionally, because of the shrinking size of the market, the use of a third-party broker cuts into the minimal profit margins. "There is no money or future in being a broker," one former broker told us. Another trend is gray-market buyers and sellers shifting to the white market.[24]

Business Models Vary

Exploit development for profit has existed since the late 1990s to early 2000s. Since then, business models and focus have shifted, and exploit development and zero-day vulnerability exploitation now involve a much more formalized process. For example, in the early days, exploit developers looked for exploitable vulnerabilities in anything, exploits tended to be more specific to the operating system, and exploit development generally stopped at the PoC level. Now, exploit developers are more customer-focused, exploits tend to be more process- and application-specific, and buyers require exploits to be fully functioning and work on multiple versions and configurations.

Some gray-market players lease, rent, contract, or license their exploits so they retain all intellectual property. A typical (usually exclusive) leasing contract is about two years. When the contract expires, the customer often has the option to re-lease the exploit. Each customer gets a specific license for the exploit, which specifies what the customer can and cannot do (although there is no way for the company or exploit developer to enforce this). Some sellers are selective about whom they sell to, so they may have only have a handful of customers to choose from.[25]

Other vulnerability research groups maintain that there is no benefit to anything other than selling, because many of the customers already share the information

---

[23] See Chapter Four of Libicki, Ablon, and Webb (2015) for more discussion of and distinction between the three markets.

[24] One expert attributed this to the white market only now being sellable because the marketing environment and perspective have shifted. In the past, one had to position oneself as a "master of the dark arts" to get customers. Once a vulnerability researcher gained traction, she or he could shift to the white market.

[25] One vulnerability research group shared that they had three to four entities to which they sell; another noted approximately the same number.

and license restrictions are difficult to enforce.[26] Additionally, because there are so few customers, there is disincentive for a vulnerability research group to try to enforce an exploit only going to one place.

In general, buyers demand exclusivity, likely for operational security requirements. Exploits that are similar (in terms of the bug class or library they target, or the exploit technique they use) are sometimes sold or leased to different customers, but generally only if the seller can reasonably determine that the discovery of one will not lead to the discovery of another. Some buyers have internal rules that cap the number of vulnerabilities they can retain per system, so they may pay an exploit developer to keep an exploit "on the shelf" for purchase or rent at a later date.

Some buyers of exploits will be specific about what they want an exploit for (e.g., a specific piece of software with a particular configuration); others may want something for a specific target, telling the exploit developers "Get me into this target system or target organization, I don't care how." Sometimes buyers are specific about the mechanics of the exploit, noting whether or not crashes are acceptable, what platforms or architectures need to be supported (e.g., 32-bit versus 64-bit), whether the exploit needs to be a man-in-the-middle exploit, or whether there are certain timing requirements.[27] Ideally, customers share what they want a vulnerability researcher to focus on because of target and operational sensitivities. This increases the return on investment for both the exploit developer and the purchaser: The former has something to focus on and a higher guarantee of a buy, and the latter gets what they want. In these cases, the vulnerability researcher might offer a menu of exploits available and leave it to the customer to choose one. Because they are not clairvoyant, exploit developers are sometimes left with exploits sitting on the shelf, acting as a "caching layer" until a customer requests the particular exploit. This risks an exploit spoiling or its vulnerabilities being discovered. One exploit development group estimated that 50 percent of its developed exploits remain on the shelf.

---

[26] These sellers might, however, have some reusable "helper code" to assist the customer in testing the exploit until the customer can write their own production code for operational use. The helper code is retained by the seller.

[27] "Man-in-the-middle" or "machine-in-the-middle" refers to an attacker who is in the middle of the legitimate sender and receiver, relaying and possibly altering the communications between the two parties.

Exploit Developers (and Exploit Development Companies) Often Supplement Their Income with Consulting and Selling Vulnerability Feeds

Despite claims that vast amounts of money can be made creating zero-day exploits,[28] few companies and organizations today focus exclusively on exploit development.[29] They usually supplement their exploit development with other businesses such as offering penetration testing services or a vulnerability feed, or selling data, supporting tools, and products.[30] Exploit development is difficult to scale, and, except for individual contractors working alone, the financial incentives are not often present.[31]

It is believed that approximately two dozen companies are in the business of selling to U.S. or U.S.-allied entities, with this number decreasing steadily.[32] Some people familiar with the white and gray markets attributed the diminishing numbers to high costs, claiming that many of those companies found that the exploit product model was not as lucrative as the service model or as publicly acceptable as bug bounties and bug hunting on the public market.[33]

---

[28] For example, Fidler, Granick, and Crenshaw (2014) estimate the size of the gray market at $4 million to $10 million. We were told by vulnerability research groups that the U.S. government invests much more than that on having products assessed and subscribing to vulnerability feeds, and less on buying exploits and zero-day vulnerabilities.

[29] One vulnerability research group estimated revenue from exploit development at 6 to 7 percent of the overall business, with most revenue coming from commercial consulting gigs and selling tools. These commercial consulting gigs can be thought of as "short lifetime bug hunting." Often, during a security assessment, a zero-day vulnerability will be discovered at a client site, and, as such, will get immediately disclosed. One vulnerability research company noted that their consulting arm finds more zero-day vulnerabilities than their research arm. This may be due to the fact that, for a researcher to find a zero-day vulnerability, she needs to set up the software, back-end database, and infrastructure before any auditing can begin; that setup can easily take a month. A consultant, however, already has the full infrastructure set up at the client site, so it is sometimes easier to find zero-day vulnerabilities there. These zero-days tend to be of specific types—often, enterprise versions (versus personal or consumer use versions) or software that only runs on a particular vertical (e.g., software specific to a law firm or health care facility).

[30] A vulnerability feed is a subscription-based model, whereby subscribers get regular information about zero-day vulnerabilities that have not yet been disclosed. Often, subscribers use the feed to test their own products against zero-day vulnerabilities to further secure them, or use the feed during penetration tests or consulting engagements to test their client's products, networks, and systems.

[31] One of the biggest reasons is that exploit developers are expensive: A company with seven or eight top-tier, full-time vulnerability researchers making in the "mid-to-high six-figures" may make $1 million to $2.5 million in a year selling exploits, but the lion's share of that revenue goes to the analysts. One company told us that 2015 was a negative payout from revenue, yet they continued to develop exploits because it is "a labor of love" that provides satisfaction beyond compensation.

[32] These companies consist of both boutique firms (with a handful of researchers) and arms of traditional large cleared defense contractors (with large numbers of researchers). One exploit developer was personally aware of more than 18 such companies just in the business of selling in the U.S. arena. The developer was also aware of a handful of other foreign companies that focused on their governments. That said, many of these companies are newer to the space, and many have only been around for a few years.

[33] One example of a company publicly changing its business model is Exodus, which in February 2016 announced that it would keep vulnerabilities for only 90 days for its customer feed, then it would disclose the vulnerability for the affected vendor to patch (Exodus Intelligence, 2016).

CHAPTER THREE

Analysis of the Data

As mentioned in Chapter One, in deciding whether to stockpile or disclose a particular vulnerability, one may want to know the following:

1. **Life status:** Is the vulnerability really a zero-day? Is it alive (publicly unknown) or dead (known to others)?
2. **Longevity:** How long will the vulnerability remain undiscovered and undisclosed to the public?
3. **Collision rate:** What is the likelihood that others will discover and disclose the vulnerability?

It may be additionally helpful to know:

4. **Cost:** What is the cost to develop an exploit for the vulnerability?

The following sections explore answers to each of these questions—in particular, what vulnerabilities are publicly unknown or known (life status), how long they live (survival probability and life expectancy), and the rate of collision (overlap). We also briefly touch on some considerations for the cost to develop an exploit. Because we used different methodologies and approaches for each section, we discuss the methods and analysis within each section.

Our dataset contains information about exploits, so when we discuss life status, life expectancy, and overlap or collision rate, we are referring to the vulnerability or vulnerabilities that the exploit is taking advantage of. An exploit dying means that one of the previously unknown vulnerabilities (if multiple exist) gets discovered.[1]

---

[1] It could also have a patch available, but at the most basic level, we define "death" as discovery by others.

1. Life Status: Is the Vulnerability Really a Zero-Day? Is It Alive (Publicly Unknown) or Dead (Known to Others)?

Common practice is to classify a vulnerability simply as alive (publicly unknown) or dead (publicly known); however, our analysis revealed that **there is more granularity to a vulnerability being either alive or dead**. There are several subcategories of each, which can make labeling a vulnerability as either alive or dead misleading and too simplistic.[2] Below, we list the various life statuses of vulnerabilities and their exploits and outline how they are classified in our dataset.

Alive: There Are Different Ways for a Vulnerability to Be Alive (Publicly Unknown)

Some vulnerabilities are publicly unknown and still actively sought out by defenders (because they reside in the latest versions of an operating system, or are in use by a large percentage of people). These are classified in our dataset as "**Living**" (n = 66).

There are vulnerabilities that will remain in a product in perpetuity because the vendor no longer maintains the code or issues updates. We classify this type of vulnerability as "**Immortal**" (n = 13). This does not necessarily mean the vulnerability has any special properties that made it immortal: It could be immortal because it was found just before the vendor stopped maintaining the codebase, and might have been found given enough time.

Dead: There Are Different Ways for a Vulnerability to Be Dead (Publicly Known)

Vulnerabilities that are known can be disclosed publicly by the researchers who found them or by another party.

When a vulnerability has been disclosed by the original vulnerability researcher, we classify it as "**Killed by BUSBY**" (n = 8). The researcher may do so to help the information security community as a whole by sharing the information, or to get credit for finding and disclosing a vulnerability that the researcher feels might be easily or imminently found by someone else.

When a vulnerability has been disclosed by another party, it is often in conjunction with a security advisory or bulletin and patch, and we classify it as "**Security Patch**" (n = 69). The security advisory contains information about the vulnerability, and may include Common Vulnerabilities and Exposures (CVEs) that describe the vulnerability and CVSS scores that detail severity. Interestingly, CVEs do not always provide accurate and complete information about the severity of the vulnerability.[3]

---

[2]   We recognize that using terms such as "dead" may be misleading, because the vast majority of cyber actions use these "dead" N-Day vulnerabilities. One expert we spoke with suggested we use the terminology "a vulnerability previously undescribed in literature," especially given that strong emotional reaction to the words *alive* and *dead* (and *weaponized*) can make it difficult to be objective and dispassionate about the topic.

[3]   It is easy to understand why vendors may not want to give out too much detail about the vulnerabilities their patches fixed. See Rescorla, 2005. For one exploit whose vulnerability died via security patch in our dataset, the

And sometimes a vulnerability is discovered and publicly disclosed in one system but remains publicly unknown—and privately exploitable—in another system.[4]

But not all vulnerabilities that are disclosed by others have a security advisory or patch. Sometimes, developers or vulnerability researchers will post a bug or vulnerability they found in a mailing list, an online blog, or a book. The poster may or may not be aware that the bug discussed is actually a security vulnerability, so there is no security advisory connected with the vulnerability. We classify these in our data as "**Publicly Shared**" (n = 6).

Other: Some Vulnerabilities Fit into Other Categories

An intriguing type of vulnerability are those that get removed through revisions to the code without being discovered or publicly disclosed as security vulnerabilities. We classify these as "**Code Refactor**" (n = 21). These vulnerabilities can still be exploited in older versions, so they are quasi-alive (zombies). However, some may see these zombie vulnerabilities as "dead" because they are no longer alive in the latest version of the software.[5]

We classified the life status of some of the exploits in our dataset as "**Uncertain**" (n = 24). These consisted of exploits whose vulnerabilities' status remained uncertain, even after extensive searches online. At the time of writing, these vulnerabilities were still being reviewed for status (i.e., the BUSBY researchers were checking them against the latest versions).

Our dataset contained vulnerabilities that are alive (publicly unknown) in one codebase but dead (publicly known) in another. For example, code that contained a vulnerability allowing a sandbox escape in a Microsoft product was ported over to a non-Microsoft product; the vulnerability was discovered and patched in the Microsoft product but remains undiscovered (and unpatched) in the non-Microsoft product.

CVE notes that an exploit could use a particular value to trigger a heap-based overflow, but fails to note that a differently crafted exploit could actually change the value of the trigger. In another case, the CVE lists the vulnerability as something that, when exploited, causes a denial of service, but the BUSBY vulnerability researchers found that it could provide privilege escalation—something much more severe.

[4] For example, one of BUSBY's exploits had a vulnerability that had been found in a 32-bit version of a system but was not exploitable. Once the 64-bit version came out, the vulnerability was exploitable. That particular vulnerability lived for more than five years before a security patch was released.

[5] Sometimes, a code refactor can turn a previous codebase into a whole new product—to the advantage or disadvantage of exploit developers. A code refactor may inadvertently change a codebase so that vulnerabilities are no longer present or exploitable; other times, a code refactor will unblock paths to previously unexploitable vulnerabilities. A product that was previously sparse may become dense with exploitable vulnerabilities, and vice versa. For example, in 2012, Rapid7 looked at the old code bases of Universal Plug and Play (UPnP)-enabled network devices that had been refactored in 2010; they showed how previous versions of UPnP-enabled devices were vulnerable and remained vulnerable. Because many systems retain old versions—due to lack of ability, resources, or awareness to upgrade—many LinkSys routers around the world still remained vulnerable. (See hdmoore, 2013.) The takeaway is that it is valuable to go back and audit old versions of code, especially (from an offensive point of view) if it is known that a certain target or sector is not likely to update.

Exploits for both of these were created, and we recorded them with the appropriate life status in our dataset.

Figure 3.1 shows the data broken down by life status, with just the categories "alive," "dead," and "other," while Figure 3.2 shows the further breakdown, with all the categories. Table 3.1 provides a summary description of each life status.

Figures 3.3 and 3.4 break down vulnerabilities found by BUSBY vulnerability researchers between 2002 and 2015. Some data (an estimated 20–30 exploits) are omit-

**Figure 3.1
Simple Breakdown of Life Status
for Our Data (n = 207)**

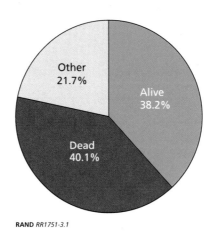

RAND RR1751-3.1

**Figure 3.2
Further Breakdown of Life Status for Our
Data (n = 207)**

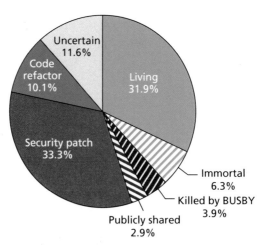

RAND RR1751-3.2

Table 3.1
Description of Various Life Statuses

Life Status	Description
Living	A publicly unknown vulnerability for current versions of the product; not found and publicly noted by anyone else (as far as it is known); those in defensive roles are likely actively looking for it.
Immortal	A publicly unknown vulnerability for the version of the product it was created for; that product is no longer maintained (so a security patch will never be issued).
Security Patch	A vulnerability found by a third party and recognized as a security vulnerability; an advisory, patch, and/or CVE has been issued.
Killed by BUSBY	A vulnerability publicly disclosed by the private entity that found it when they realized that vulnerability was about to be found, or when they wanted to use a particular vulnerability as a teaching tool or for marketing purposes.
Publicly Shared	A vulnerability found by a third party and publicly discussed, but *not* publicly recognized as a security vulnerability; no advisory, patch, and/or CVE issued.
Code Refactor	A likely publicly unknown vulnerability for past versions of a product that is no longer exploitable in current versions due to code revisions; the product is still maintained (so a security patch sometime in the future is still possible for the past versions).

Figure 3.3
Vulnerabilities Found by BUSBY Vulnerability Researchers Each Year (n = 207)

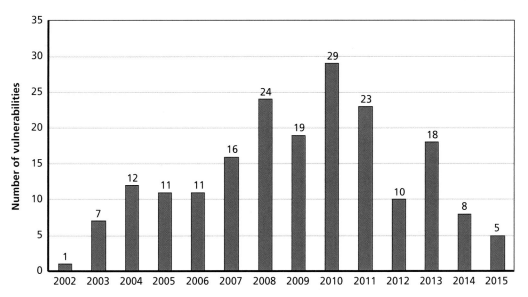

Figure 3.4
Vulnerabilities Found by BUSBY Each Year, by Current Life Status (n = 207)

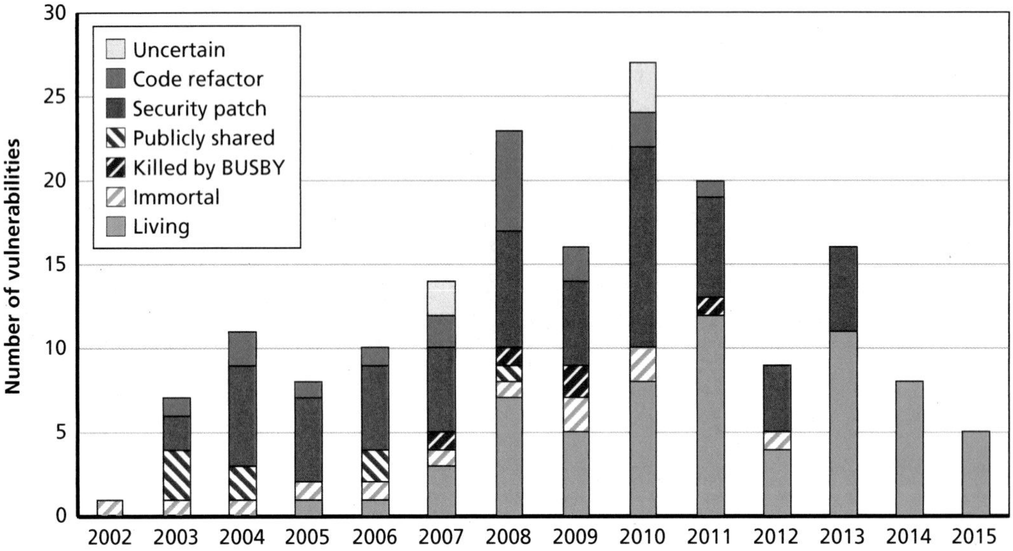

ted in the latter years (and all data for those found in 2016 are omitted) because of sensitivities of current operations.

Not all vulnerabilities used for exploits were found by the vulnerability researchers associated with our dataset. Sometimes a vulnerability was purchased from a third-party researcher to help complete an exploit (recall that an exploit may rely on multiple vulnerabilities to be fully functioning).[6] In our dataset, nine of the exploits (approximately 4 percent) were purchased from an outside third-party researcher. Two were Code Refactored, and the rest died (one was publicly disclosed, and the other had security patches). Of those that died, the average age of the exploit created from them was slightly less than a year and a half (521 days).

Some years saw more vulnerabilities die than others. Vulnerabilities that were discovered by vulnerability researchers in 2010 fared worse than those found in any other year. This might be explained by new mitigations starting in 2011 that countered vulnerabilities from previous years (e.g., stack cookies), causing the vulnerability researchers to change exploitation techniques.[7]

---

[6] For example, an exploit developer might need an information leak vulnerability in some part of a kernel in order to bypass a mitigation like ASLR to continue with the rest of exploitation.

[7] See Appendix C, "How Mitigations Have Affected Exploitability: Heap Versus Stack Exploitation Case Study," for some data analysis on shifts in exploitation methods (e.g., between stack-based memory corruption vulnerabilities and heap-based memory corruption vulnerabilities).

How Do Vulnerabilities Die?

While we do not have data on how deaths occurred—of our vulnerabilities, or other vulnerabilities used to create fully functioning exploits—we do have qualitative assessments from several vulnerability researchers and individuals with whom we spoke. They said the majority of their exploits die (i.e., their vulnerabilities became known) due to code churn and, less commonly, to independent rediscovery by a vulnerability researcher performing a code audit. None we spoke to believed that their vulnerabilities or exploits died or were discovered due to use by a customer in some operational campaign, or by information leakage (e.g., via Wikileaks or Shadow Brokers releasing information). That said, vulnerability researchers are also not privy to what a customer does with their exploit—i.e., when they use it, how they use it, or whether they use it at all.

Due to sensitivity, operational, or other reasons, often a customer cannot disclose exactly what product or system they want an exploit for. As such, vulnerability researchers make educated guesses about a customer's needs. While the ideal is for all exploits developed to be sold to customers, there are cases where exploits die while sitting on the shelf. One vulnerability research team told us that 99 percent of their exploits go to customers. Another team put the number at closer to 50 percent, and a third individual with experience in the exploit sales business could not recall any time when an exploit sat unused.

2. Longevity: How Long Will the Vulnerability Remain Undiscovered and Undisclosed to the Public?

Determining how long an exploit might live before its vulnerability or vulnerabilities are detected—as well as which exploits live the shortest and the longest—could help exploit developers adjust their business models and help defensive penetration testers or offensive operators plan their engagements.

We sought to understand the expected life of an exploit. **We found that exploits are expected to live 6.9 years on average and have a median survival time of 5.07 years. We define a short lifetime to be death (or its vulnerabilities become known and publicly disclosed) within 1.51 years, corresponding to the 25th percentile of the survival distribution, and a long lifetime to be at least 9.53 years, corresponding to the 75th percentile.**

For this part of our analysis, we reduced our dataset from the full set (n = 207) to just those exploits that were alive (living) or dead (security patch or public disclosure) *and* that had a date of birth (n = 127).[8]

---

[8]   Seven of our exploits that died had no birthdate recorded, as their vulnerabilities were purchased by a third party. We do have date of maturity for those exploits (i.e., the date when a fully functional exploit had been created), but to ensure uniformity over our data, we elected to exclude these exploits. We also considered including

Table F.1 in Appendix F, "Additional Figures and Tables," provides a breakdown of the various characteristics of the exploits.

Survival Analysis

We sought to describe the distribution of the length of time from birth to death of the 127 exploits described above, to assess the effects of several exploit-level characteristics on the risk of death, and to calculate the expected lifespan of exploits overall and by their characteristics. This requires analytic methods that account for differences in the amount of time we were able to observe each exploit. Some exploits in our data were born as early as 2003, allowing more than ten years of observation time in which we might observe its death. Others were born just a year or two before our analysis. We therefore cannot observe the full lifespan of each exploit; those that remain undetected at the end of the study period are referred to as *censored*. Censored data are common in health studies, where investigators may not get to observe each patient until some event of interest. In our study, censoring occurs administratively due to the end of study data collection. More generally, censoring can occur whenever subjects in a time-to-event study are lost to follow-up, even midway through a study, perhaps when they move away or choose to withdraw. A suite of statistical methods exists for the analysis of censored time-to-event data, collectively referred to as survival analysis.

Describing Survivorship with Kaplan-Meier Estimation

Kaplan-Meier analysis is used to estimate a population survival curve from a sample and the probability of surviving from some event of interest (e.g., someone having a heart attack) as a function of time. In our case, the event of interest is the death of an exploit as a result of its vulnerability being discovered and disclosed. Kaplan-Meier accommodates censored data, in which the event of interest (death or discovery) has not occurred for all of the sample's observations (exploits) before the end of the study period.[9]

To graphically depict the survival experience of the exploits in our sample, we constructed the Kaplan-Meier survival curve both overall and in groups defined by exploit characteristics. The survival curve plots the probability of a zero-day vulnerability remaining living along the vertical axis as a function of the time since birth, shown along the horizontal axis. From these plots, we obtained the median survival time—

---

exploits that had a life status of Immortal; however, because survival analysis and life expectancy analysis are typically done on humans or things that are all expected to die or fail at some point, we removed the immortal exploits.

[9]   Kaplan-Meier analysis, and survival analysis generally, assumes that censoring is not informative—that is, that the exploits that are censored (still alive at the end of the study) have a similar survival experience over time as those we do observe to die. For more information on Kaplan-Meier, see Bland (1998); Lam (no date); and Goel et al. (2010).

that is, the time by which half of the sample had died. We also used the Kaplan-Meier plot to identify specific quantiles of the survival time distribution to define thresholds for what might be considered a "short" or "long" lifespan. In our case, we chose the 25th and 75th percentiles, or times by which 25 percent and 75 percent had died, as thresholds for long and short lifetimes.

We estimated the expected life span of the exploits in our sample, both overall and by exploit characteristics, by calculating the area beneath the survival curve. However, as is visible in our Kaplan-Meier plots (Figures 3.5 and 3.6), the survival curves we estimated are not "finished yet." That is, we did not have sufficient follow-up time on each exploit to observe its death, and for that reason, the survival curves do not descend fully to the x-axis, corresponding to zero survival probability (i.e., the lines end horizontally rather than vertically). For this reason, the area beneath those curves is undefined. To allow estimation of the expected lifespan, we employed a different type of survival regression model, which places a distributional assumption on the data that can allow us to extrapolate the remaining part of the function until it reaches sufficiently close to zero as to obtain an appropriate estimate of the area beneath it. We investigated several common parametric survival model types that might be of use, and chose the one that best suited the characteristics of our data.

Finally, to assess the effect of individual characteristics on the risk of death of an exploit, we estimated Cox Proportional Hazards survival regression models. This modeling strategy is one that places fewer assumptions on the data than the parametric modeling we used to generate life expectancies, and allows more flexibility in covariate adjustment than does the comparison of Kaplan-Meier curves.

Figure 3.5 shows the Kaplan-Meier survival probability estimates, calculated using all the data, and without stratifying by characteristic. The gray band surrounding the blue line shows the pointwise 95 percent confidence band.[10] The confidence interval is smaller for exploits that died young (few years since birth), because there were more data points to draw from, providing greater precision in the estimate of survival probability.[11]

After initial detection, any given exploit (and thus its vulnerabilities) has a median survival time of 5.07 years (95 percent confidence interval: 3.71, 7.55). This means that any given exploit within our dataset had a 50 percent probability of surviving approximately five years before its vulnerabilities were publicly discovered and disclosed. Fur-

---

[10] One can interpret confidence intervals as follows: For any given age (years since birth), we are 95 percent confident that the true survival probability falls in the gray shaded area.

[11] All exploits lived at least a short period of time, so the relatively high precision yields a tighter confidence interval. Compare this with the larger confidence intervals as the years since birth get higher; only a few exploits lived this long, causing a wider confidence interval.

Figure 3.5
Kaplan-Meier Survival Probability Estimates (n = 127)

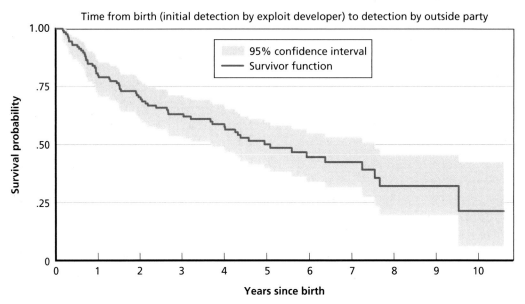

thermore, there is a relatively sharp decline in the survival probability in an exploit's early years.[12]

We further sought to define reasonable thresholds for characterizing exploits as being "young" exploits or "old" exploits. We obtained the 25th and 75th percentiles of the survival time distribution, the times by which 25 percent and 75 percent of the exploits have died, respectively.[13] Using these quantiles, we define exploits as having a short lifespan if they die at or before 1.51 years, corresponding to the time at which only 25 percent have died. Exploits that survive at least 9.53 years have lived as long or longer than 75 percent of the sample, and so are considered to have had a long lifespan.

To assess whether survival differs according to characteristics specific to an exploit, we plotted Kaplan-Meier curves separately for the following four characteristics of an exploit: vulnerability type, platform affected, source code type, and exploit class type. Appendix H, "Glossary," provides definitions and additional information about the various vulnerability types and exploit class types:[14]

---

[12]   The life table (Table F.2) and smoothed hazard function corresponding to the life table plot (Figure F.2) show this.

[13]   We acknowledge that we could have just as easily chosen the top and bottom 10 percent, or some other number.

[14]   Some characteristics show up as "mixed" or "other." "Mixed" characteristics indicate exploits that rely on multiple vulnerabilities chained together (for vulnerability type), multiple platforms, multiple source code types, or

1. **Vulnerability type:** Memory Corruption, Memory Mismanagement, Logic, Mixed or Other
2. **Platform affected:** Linux, OSX, Open Source, PHP, Unix-based (excluding Linux), Windows, Mixed, Other
3. **Source code type:** Open, Closed, Mixed
4. **Exploit class type:** Client-side, Local, Remote, Mixed, Other.

We computed the log-rank test for each characteristic (vulnerability type, platform affected, source code type, and exploit class type), testing for differences in the Kaplan-Meier curves across levels (e.g., open, closed, or mixed for source code type characteristic). Figure 3.6 shows the Kaplan-Meier curves for each characteristic and the log-rank test p-value from comparing the curves within each panel to see whether curves are statistically different.[15]

We did not observe statistically significant differences in survival across any of our four characteristics. Detecting differences across the curves is made more difficult when a characteristic has many levels, because the number of failures becomes increasingly small as the data are separated into more and more levels.

Curves in the **vulnerability type** panel do not show signs of meaningful differences across their levels (p = 0.597). For **platform affected**, the large number of categories is difficult to detect differences across levels. We explored comparing Linux-based exploits to all others combined, as the plot suggests that the Linux exploits may tend to survive longer, though that difference had a nonsignificant p-value of 0.357. In the **source type** plot, the curves for open and closed source exploits are nearly identical, consistent with findings by other investigators (p = 0.729) (Altkinkemer, Reese, and Sridhar, 2008; Schryen and Rich, 2010). The curve for the "mixed" category in this panel does not descend at all, as we observed no deaths among "mixed" exploits. Finally, in the **class type** panel, we are again challenged by comparing across a large number of categories, and find no significant difference in survival across class types (p = 0.293). However, there is a suggestion in the figure that collapsing this variable into two categories—grouping client-side and remote exploits together and comparing them against the combined local, mixed, and other exploits—may produce groups that differ. As an exploration, we formed these groups and found that they did not differ significantly (p = 0.068, plot not shown), though the p-value is low enough as to suggest this as a potential question for further study.

The lack of observation of statistically significant differences in survival across our four characteristics may be because there really are no differences, though it also might

---

multiple exploit classes. "Other" characteristics indicate categories that had too few data points to be considered for this analysis on their own, so they were combined.

[15]   Curves that end in a horizontal line indicate that the last observed value was alive; curves that end in a vertical line indicate that the last observed value was death (i.e., public disclosure) and that there is no evidence of continued survival for that particular element.

Figure 3.6
Kaplan-Meier Curves for Vulnerability Type, Platform Affected, Source Code Type, and Exploit Class Type (n = 127)

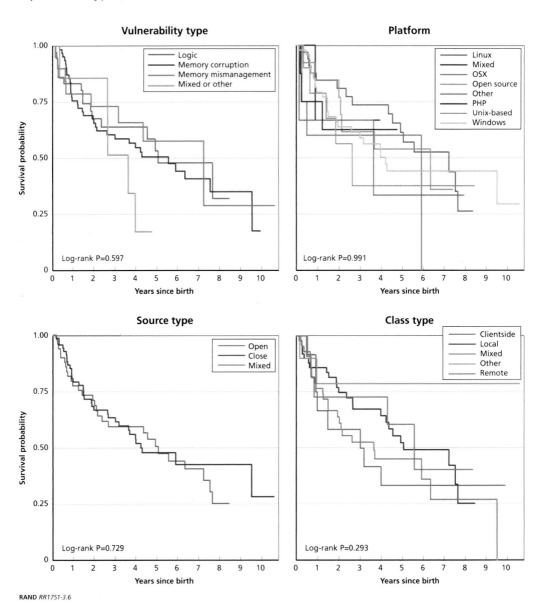

be due to a lack of data. As such, **our analysis provides guidance on what hypotheses to test in future analyses—in particular, to examine longevity of vulnerabilities for Linux compared with other platforms; to confirm the similarity of longevity of vulnerabilities for open and closed source code type; and to investigate any significance of grouping client-side and remote exploits together compared against a grouping of local, mixed, and other exploits.**

Life Expectancy

In addition to exploring median, long, and short survival times, we wanted to examine the survival experience of our data in a different way: life expectancy. Life expectancy can be estimated directly from a survival curve by calculating the area beneath it. This is relatively simple, provided we observe the failure of each subject (i.e., the discovery/death of all zero-day exploits), bringing the curve down to zero. However, our Kaplan-Meier curves do not reach zero because we did not observe the death of all 127 exploits, making the area under the Kaplan-Meier curve impossible to calculate directly.

In cases like this, one can use other survival analysis tools that allow a complete survival curve to be estimated, even when the last observation time is censored, provided we are willing to impose parametric assumptions on the survival time distribution. We examined exponential, Weibull, and log-normal survival models for their fit to our data by comparing their estimated survival plots to the Kaplan-Meier plots we had already constructed.[16] Each of these models fit our data reasonably well, providing curves that fell within the confidence band in the overall Kaplan-Meier curve in Figure 3.5. However, we felt that the exponential model was the best choice for our data, based on its assumption of a constant hazard function, which our data appear to exhibit. Further details about the hazard function and plots of our unadjusted hazard estimates and parametric model comparisons can be found in Appendix F, "Additional Figures and Tables."

Using our exponential regression model, we were able to obtain a model-based survival curve estimate that extends arbitrarily close to the x-axis, allowing us to calculate the area beneath it, which is our unadjusted estimate of the life expectancy of an average exploit in our sample. We fit four additional exponential models, adjusting for each of the four characteristics of an exploit (vulnerability type, platform affected, source type, and exploit class type) one at a time, in order to obtain life expectancies for exploits within each level of the characteristics. Table 3.2 presents life expectancy estimates, both overall and by specific characteristics.

The life expectancies complement the results from the Kaplan-Meier curves in an intuitive way; the steeper the descent of the survivor function, the shorter we expect the estimated life expectancy to be. Additionally, the more events we observe as downward "steps" on the Kaplan-Meier plot, the narrower the confidence interval around

---

[16]   See Figure F.1 in Appendix F, "Additional Figures and Tables."

Table 3.2
Life Expectancy Estimates Overall and by Exploit
Characteristics Obtained from Unadjusted Exponential
Survival Models (n = 127)

Exploit Characteristic	Exponential Model-Based Life Expectancy Estimates (95% CI)
Overall	6.90 (5.39, 8.84)
Vulnerability Type	
Logic	7.20 (4.41, 11.75)
Memory Corruption	6.75 (4.83, 9.45)
Memory Mismanagement	8.81 (4.41, 17.55)
Mixed or Other	3.92 (1.63, 9.40)
Platform Affected	
Linux	8.62 (5.28, 14.06)
Mixed	6.90 (0.98, 42.63)
OSX	5.36 (2.02, 14.27)
Open Source	7.32 (3.49, 15.32)
Other	5.90 (1.48, 23.25)
PHP	5.59 (1.81, 17.27)
Unix-based	5.95 (2.48, 14.27)
Windows	6.36 (4.30, 9.42)
Source Type	
Open	6.51 (4.50, 9.43)
Closed	6.93 (4.95, 9.70)
Mixed	–
Exploit Class Type	
Client-side	5.16 (2.58, 10.32)
Local	7.63 (5.12, 11.39)
Mixed	8.71 (3.63, 20.75)
Other	21.48 (5.43, 59.36)
Remote	5.14 (3.45, 7.67)

the life expectancy estimate. Precision in our life expectancy estimates varies markedly across characteristics; categories in which we observed many events provide tighter confidence intervals around their point estimates (for example, Windows vulnerabilities and remote and local exploits), and categories with very few observed events (for example, see the "mixed" and "other" exploit types) had much wider confidence intervals.[17] Assuming that what we have is a representative sample of exploits, we find that the average exploit (and thus its vulnerabilities) is expected to live 6.90 years (with 95 percent confidence interval: 5.39 to 8.84 years).[18]

Proportional Hazards Regression Modeling

To assess whether any particular characteristic of an exploit contributes to a lower or higher probability of death, leading to longer or shorter lifespans, we fit Cox proportional hazards survival models.

We used Cox proportional hazards regression modeling to estimate the hazard ratio associated with each level of each characteristic compared with its referent category. We fit separate unadjusted models for each of our four characteristics, as well as a fully adjusted model adjusting for all four characteristics simultaneously, and a partially adjusted model that excluded platform affected. Table F.3 and the surrounding text in Appendix F, "Additional Figures and Tables," provide more details about the methodologies used and values for each model.

Consistent with the Kaplan-Meier results, there does not appear to be any "smoking gun" characteristics that may indicate a long or short life, though our findings are useful for hypothesis generation. A "smoking gun" characteristic would have suggested that a vulnerability or its exploit might last a long or short time, perhaps aiding those who deal with the vulnerabilities equities process refine what should be kept and what should be publicly released. For example, if all exploits that rely on memory corruption vulnerabilities are statistically shown to have lower survival probabilities over time, then perhaps those should be the types of vulnerabilities that get publicly disclosed and patched (i.e., not stockpiled), because those wishing to exploit them for their own operations may get a short time to use with them, and more people may be at risk given the quick discovery rate.[19] Similarly, if a particular type or aspect of a vulnerability indicates a long time, stockpiling may be a justifiable option.

With our data, for each characteristic, the p-values from Wald tests of regression parameter estimates are too high to infer any significant differences across any of its

---

[17] Confidence intervals give a sense of how precisely we have estimated each individual life expectancy. That is, we are able to state with 95 percent confidence that the life expectancies for each characteristic lie within the confidence intervals as shown.

[18] A 95 percent confidence interval of 5.39 to 8.84 years means we are 95 percent confident that the average lifespan of exploits like those in our sample is between 5.39 and 8.84 years.

[19] Of course, it depends on the platform and target system affected. It might be the case that, even if a vulnerability is quick to exploit and has a short lifetime, a short time of using it could prove valuable.

levels, with or without adjustment for the other characteristics. Without more data, we cannot statistically determine whether any characteristic of an exploit indicates a long or short life. The high p-values may be a result of a true absence of effect, or a result of a small number of observed deaths, owing to our small sample size. More data and longer follow-up time may provide statistically significant solutions in further study.

3. Collision Rate: What Is the Likelihood That Others Will Discover and Disclose the Vulnerability?

Just as understanding the longevity of a particular vulnerability is valuable, so is knowing how likely it is that a vulnerability will be discovered by another researcher, regardless of how long the vulnerability has already been alive.

A high collision rate might indicate that vulnerabilities found by private researchers and public bug hunters are relatively easy to detect, strengthening an argument for disclosing any vulnerability found.[20] Similarly, a low collision rate might indicate that vulnerabilities found by one researcher will remain undetected by other researchers.

Alternatively, vulnerabilities that are seemingly difficult to detect and deeply buried in a code base could yield a high overlap if multiple vulnerability researchers use the same bug-hunting techniques.[21]

An organization that holds vulnerabilities or exploits likely assesses its stockpile at regular time periods, removing those that have been publicly discovered and disclosed and only retaining those that are still alive or potentially useful as zero-days. If newly dead exploits are thrown out at regular time periods, then the percentage of those dead at the end of each time period represents the amount of overlap, or the collision rate.

Literature on collision rate focuses mostly on vulnerabilities reported to vulnerability reward programs or publicly found and reported within a code base. Finifter, Akhawe, and Wagner (2013) found that roughly 2.25–5 percent of all vulnerabilities reported to vulnerability reward programs had been discovered by others. Past RAND rough order-of-magnitude estimates put the probability that a vulnerability is discovered by two parties within a year at approximately 10 percent (Libicki, Ablon,

---

[20] A codebase or product that has a lot of vulnerabilities discovered (i.e., high overlap and high quantity) does not necessarily mean that specific codebase or product is particularly bad or the worst offender: Market share can steer bug hunters and vulnerability researchers to look in certain codebases. Some research (Maillart et al., 2016) has shown that bug hunters often jump from product to product looking for the fastest (and sometimes cheapest) payout.

[21] Often, overlap of vulnerabilities in a code base lead to a discussion of sparseness versus denseness and depletion of vulnerabilities. This is a rich debate that many have spoken and written about. Schneier (2014) believes that vulnerabilities are plentiful (which one might interpret as dense), and as such the overlap is relatively small; Geer (2014) states that vulnerabilities are sparse enough for the U.S. government to corner the bug-buying market. Ozment and Schechter (2006) argue that the density of vulnerabilities in the OpenBSD operating system ranged from 0 to 0.033 vulnerabilities reported per 1,000 lines of code.

and Webb, 2015). Researchers in 2015 created a heuristic model that found a 9 percent overlap in non-security-tested software and 0.08 percent in more secure software (Moussouris and Siegel, 2015).

In our dataset, approximately 40 percent of the exploits were detected and publicly disclosed. We calculated this value by accumulating and keeping all exploits over the 14-year span of the dataset, regardless of whether or not an exploit or vulnerability had died.

But an organization would likely flush dead vulnerabilities from a stockpile in regular time intervals. Taking 365 days and 90 days as the likely time intervals (as well as 30 days and 1 day intervals), we performed sensitivity analysis on our data, to assess the percentage of vulnerabilities that died in certain time intervals. In each time period, we removed those that had died in the previous interval. We separated each exploit into four main categories: (1) Living, (2) Code Refactor, (3) Dead, and (4) Unknown. Collisions are represented by those exploits that are dead at the end of a particular time interval. **Collision rates change significantly depending on the interval time. While we found a ~40 percent collision rate over the 14-year span of our data, narrowing the time intervals resulted in a 5.76 percent collision rate (median value) for a 365-day time interval (6.79 percent standard deviation), and an 0.87 percent collision rate (median value) for a 90-day time interval (5.3 percent standard deviation). In other words, for a given stockpile of zero-day vulnerabilities, after a year approximately 5.7 percent have been discovered and disclosed by others.**[22]

Figure 3.7, and Figure F.3 and Table F.4 in Appendix F, "Additional Figures and Tables," show the values.

Timing of Collisions with the Same Vulnerability

One may additionally want to consider *how long* the vulnerability was known only to the private entity before discovery and disclosure to the public world, or, with our data, how long before our privately known vulnerabilities were found and disclosed publicly.

While it is true that many—or even most, as some might argue—uses of exploits are for vulnerabilities that have already been discovered and are no longer considered zero-day (Bilge and Dumitras, 2012), knowing the likelihood that a zero-day will remain a zero-day, and for how long, might be useful. In particular, those who rely on zero-day exploits for offensive or defensive purposes, such as penetration testing or trying out a new detection tool, may want to know how long they can expect to go undetected by their target during a campaign. Vulnerability researchers and exploit

---

[22] While we analyzed time intervals of 365, 90, 30, and 1 days, we provide results for only the 365- and 90-day time intervals. We calculated values by taking the median percentage of deaths across each time interval. As the windows get smaller, there are several windows in which no event occurred, thus driving the median value to zero. The median value was zero for both the 30-day and 1-day time intervals.

Figure 3.7
Vulnerability Types over Time (n = 192)

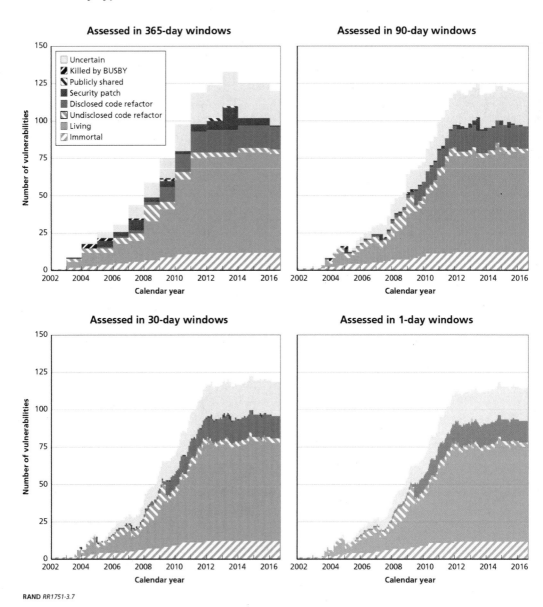

developers may want to know something about how long their exploits generally last for business or marketing purposes.[23]

We examined those vulnerabilities that were discovered by someone else in order to investigate the probability of collision and to examine the decay rate. For our data,

---

[23] For example, use the data to set prices or inform customers of expected capabilities.

"discovered by someone else" translates to a life status of "Security Patch" or "Publicly Shared," for which we have both birth and death dates.[24]

Figure 3.8 shows the amount of time between when a vulnerability used in a BUSBY exploit was found by the BUSBY vulnerability researchers and when it was found and disclosed to the public by an independent third party.

Each shaded diagonal region represents one year: the bottom shaded diagonal region (labeled 1) contains points plotted for exploits that were discovered and disclosed by someone other than BUSBY within one year after initial discovery by BUSBY. Each diagonal region above the first is labeled on the left side with the number of years

Figure 3.8
Timing of Overlap Between When a Vulnerability Was Found by Two Independent Parties (2002–2016) (n = 63)

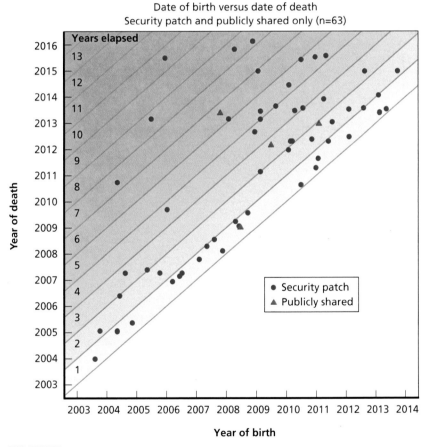

[24] While "Code Refactor" and "Killed by BUSBY" are also types of death, they do not indicate that the vulnerability was found (in the case of Code Refactor) or found by anyone else (in the case of Killed by BUSBY).

elapsed between initial discovery by BUSBY and subsequent independent discovery and disclosure.[25] Therefore, the fewer number of points in the higher diagonal bands is artificially lower than what the complete plot would display, if we had had additional follow-up time available.

Because this analysis does not take into account censoring, we cannot make any concrete conclusions about the rate of overlap. That said, **one could make the qualified observation that, in the 2002–2016 time frame, the data appear to show that, for exploits that die (i.e., are found by independent parties), death seems to happen relatively quickly and often within the first year.** The plot may also suggest that the rate of discovery is not consistent each year. For example, it appears that, beginning in 2008, a number of exploits of BUSBY vulnerability researchers lived longer than those found in previous years. The reason why is unclear: It could be that the researchers developed a new technique, or discovered a new trove of exploits that were different from the ones before, mitigations that prevented exploits from living a long time pre-2008 were countered, a new hire to the team had the ability to find vulnerabilities deep in code or in products already heavily scored, or some other unknown reason. To be clear, this is speculation: It may well be that in the future, a batch of vulnerabilities will be independently discovered and disclosed that were found by BUSBY back in 2005, which could cast doubt on the list of possible reasons.

4. Cost: What Is the Cost to Develop an Exploit for the Vulnerability?

Planning for a Stockpile: Understanding the Cost of Maintaining Ready-to-Use Exploits

If a person or organization wants to keep a stockpile of vulnerabilities ready for use, it is useful to know what it might take to replenish and maintain a full stockpile—in particular, the cost to develop an exploit, and whether in-sourcing or out-sourcing is the best option.[26]

The cost and, relatedly, value or price of an exploit can rely on many factors, which may influence cost in advance of or concurrently with exploit development. These factors include the time to find a viable zero-day vulnerability (research time), the time to develop an exploit to take advantage of the zero-day vulnerability (exploit development time), the cost of purchasing or acquiring a device or code for review, the time to set up a test lab and the cost to purchase the appropriate infrastructure or tools required

---

[25] Our chart shows births occurring through 2013, but this does not mean BUSBY analysts stopped finding and exploiting vulnerabilities that year. Rather, we did not have birth dates to calculate this. There are also some BUSBY exploits for 2014, 2015, and 2016 not included in our dataset because of additional operational sensitivities. The dataset also included five vulnerabilities sold to BUSBY by outside third parties in 2014 and beyond—all of which have died—so we are unable to determine the dates that those exploits were found.

[26] Certainly, there are many times when the use or usefulness of an exploit does not rely on its vulnerabilities being zero-day. But for the sake of argument, we consider the cases where someone would want to have zero-days.

for testing and analysis, the time to integrate a particular exploit into other ongoing operations, the salaries of the researchers involved in developing the exploit, the churn of the codebase (i.e., the likelihood for having to revisit the exploit and update it to new versions of the code to maintain a capability), the time a ready-to-go exploit sits unused, and supply and demand of an exploit for a particular platform or codebase.[27] Additional value can come from a vulnerability's uniqueness (e.g., it is the only vulnerability found in a specific product) or the need and timeline of the customer.

Benefits come from an exploit having a long enough lifetime to be of use to a customer. Ideally, an exploit development organization would look for ways to decrease the costs and increase the benefits.

Costs and Benefits of Finding Zero-Day Vulnerabilities and Developing Exploits from Them

In addition to dates of when a vulnerability had first been discovered privately (birth date), and when the vulnerability had been publicly discovered (death date), our data also included the date when a fully functioning exploit had been developed (mature date). Thus, we examined the length of time to develop an exploit as the time between birth and maturity.[28] Figure 3.9 shows the frequency counts of time to develop an exploit for our data.[29]

We found that exploit development time ranges, but is generally relatively short. In our data, 71 percent of the exploits were developed in a month (31 days or less), almost a third (31.44 percent) were developed in a week or less, and only 10 percent took more than 90 days to exploit.[30] The majority of exploits in our

---

[27] For example, the FBI reportedly spent approximately $1 million for the technique (which many suspect was a zero-day) used to unlock an iPhone (Hosenball, 2016). The high demand to unlock the iPhone likely drove up the cost.

[28] Our data did not include how long it took for a vulnerability to be initially discovered (i.e., research time), though we spoke to several people involved in vulnerability research and exploit development. We learned that the time to find a vulnerability is generally longer than the time to create a fully functioning exploit. Thus, once a vulnerability is found, it may likely be relatively quick to develop a fully functioning exploit. Granted, one needs to ensure that the infrastructure to test exists, and that may take longer to set up. See Appendix E, "Purchasing a Zero-Day Exploit: Cost and Pricing Considerations," for more discussion.

[29] There were no outstanding trends for those exploits (n = 16) that had an exploit development time of more than 90 days: Over 56 percent are still unknown (with one Immortal, and one Code Refactor), and roughly 31 percent are known and have had security patches. 56 percent were memory corruption vulnerabilities (split between stack and heap overflows). In terms of type of exploit, 50 percent were remote exploits, 25 percent local, roughly 18.75 percent client-side, and 6 percent dependent. Almost 69 percent were based on the Windows platform. The vulnerabilities were discovered between 2005 and 2014, with the majority found in 2011.

[30] Approximately 3 percent took longer than a year—with two vulnerabilities taking 2 and 2.5 years to develop exploits for. The first was exploited in 2007 and is of uncertain life status. The second was exploited in 2010 and is Immortal, as it is in a codebase that is no longer maintained. Both cases involved a remote exploit using memory corruption (heap overflow) vulnerabilities within Windows. The long time to develop an exploit was due to reliability issues.

Figure 3.9
Frequency Count of Time to Develop an Exploit (n = 159)

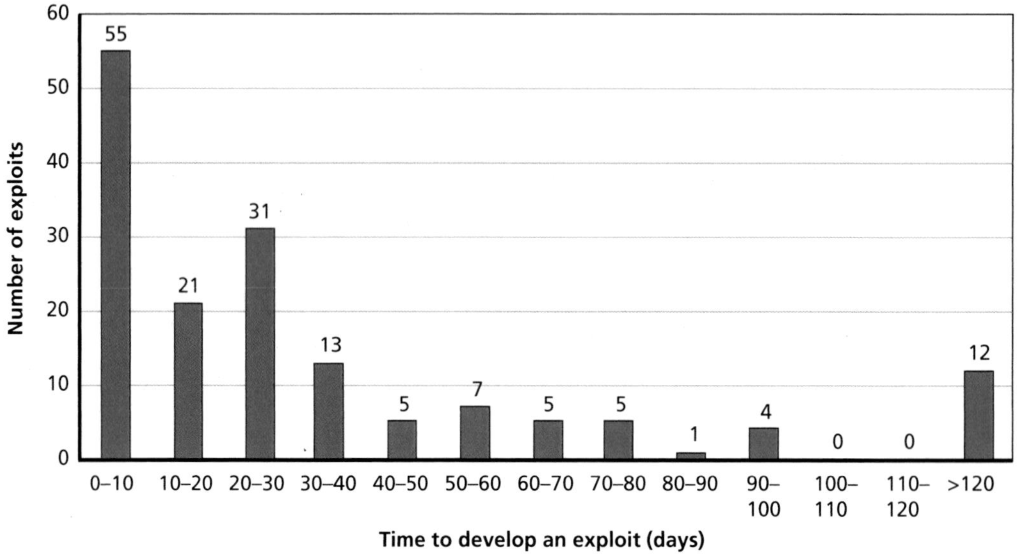

dataset took between 6 and 37 days to become fully functional (with a median of 22 days, minimum of 1 day, and maximum of 955 days).

The relatively fast exploit development time may be due, in part, to the same vulnerability researchers exploiting the same types of vulnerabilities or platforms. For example, someone who is an expert at exploiting Apple's iOS will likely have primitives (building blocks of an exploit) to rely on, so after a vulnerability is found, exploitation may be faster than someone who is new to Apple's iOS.

A long timeline to exploit could be due to a number of reasons: (1) reliability issues, as was the case for the previous examples mentioned,[31] (2) the need to chain multiple vulnerabilities together to create an exploit, (3) a customer requirement for the exploit to work on multiple versions, and (4) the vulnerability temporarily being deemed unimportant and set aside.

A long exploitation period does not necessarily mean that someone was working on the exploit the entire time: It could be that an analyst found a vulnerability, put some time into trying to exploit it, and, if it was not immediately or easily exploited within a month or certain time frame, either passing it on to another exploit developer or putting it "on the shelf" for several months until a blocker bug had been fixed or the vulnerability became more important to a customer (e.g., when a customer asked for an exploit to be developed in a particular product, no matter how long it took).

---

[31] For one, the exploit kept working well in the lab, but not in the wild.

We also evaluated exploit development time compared with lifetime (from matured to died) and by different characteristics. Similar to our finding that no characteristic of an exploit indicated a statistically significant level a long or short life, we found that time to develop an exploit did not have a bearing on how long the exploit lived and that no characteristic of an exploit indicated a long or short time to develop an exploit.[32]

For some initial analysis of cost to develop an exploit, see Appendix E, "Purchasing a Zero-Day Exploit: Cost and Pricing Considerations," for more discussion.

---

[32] As in the survival analysis, we examined vulnerability type, platform affected, source type, and exploit class. We also examined by life status.

CHAPTER FOUR

Conclusions and Implications

The value of investigating zero-day vulnerabilities is that successful findings or remaining unanswered questions can help indicate optimal areas of research for both defenders and for those offensively focused.

Our research yields several findings, two of which we highlight up front:

1. Exploits and their underlying vulnerabilities have a rather long average life expectancy (6.9 years).
2. For a given stockpile of zero-day vulnerabilities, after a year, approximately 5.7 percent have been discovered by an outside entity.

These findings imply that stockpiling maybe smart for those offensively focused, and technically sophisticated vulnerability researchers likely want to stockpile the vulnerabilities they find, rather than disclose them. Defenders will always be vulnerable to zero-day vulnerabilities, and likely will always want to disclose and patch a vulnerability upon discovery. We discuss all of our findings, and their implications for defense and offense, below.

Finding #1: Declaring a vulnerability as alive (publicly unknown) or dead (publicly known) may be misleading and too simplistic

Common practice is to classify a vulnerability simply as alive (publicly unknown) or dead (publicly known). However, our analysis revealed that there are several subcategories of each, which can make labeling a vulnerability as either alive or dead to be misleading and too simplistic. We found that vulnerabilities can exist in a quasi-dead state due to code refactoring, that vulnerabilities can die due to several reasons, and that vulnerabilities are dynamic—something that is exploitable one day may not be the next (and vice versa). Furthermore, in the course of investigating life statuses for our vulnerabilities, we found that CVEs do not always provide accurate and complete information about the severity of a vulnerability.

Implications for Defense

Oversimplifying vulnerabilities as either alive (publicly unknown) or dead (publicly known) may be creating a barrier for vulnerability-detection efforts.

"End-of-life" products can have dormant (i.e., immortal) vulnerabilities in them, so vendors and defenders should make efforts to phase out the software and encourage upgrading to new versions. Similar efforts should be made to search previous versions of code bases—unsupported or not—that have a high probability of still being in use (e.g., in industrial control systems) for vulnerabilities. Because end-of-life code bases remain relatively static, every vulnerability found would decrease the total number of bugs.

Implications for Offense

While potentially of limited use, vulnerabilities that are immortal or code refactored may still be of value for operations, depending on what system or target they reside in, and researchers should consider regularly revisiting vulnerabilities they had once found to be unexploitable.

Finding #2: Exploits have an average life expectancy of 6.9 years after initial discovery, but roughly 25 percent of exploits will not survive for more than a year and a half, and another 25 percent will survive more than 9.5 years

After initial discovery by a vulnerability researcher, exploits have an average life expectancy of 6.9 years (specifically, 2,521 days), and we estimate with 95 percent confidence that any given exploit will live between 5.39 and 8.84 years. Only 25 percent of vulnerabilities do not survive to 1.51 years, and only 25 percent live more than 9.5 years. The relatively long life expectancy of 6.9 years means that most zero-day vulnerabilities— in particular the ones for which exploits are created for private use (i.e., in the gray markets)—are likely old.

While our data show that a "short life" for a vulnerability is 1.5 years, this might be long enough for most vulnerability researchers. One exploit development team told us that they actually prefer their vulnerabilities to die after 18 months (via code churn, not independent co-discovery) in order to continue doing business selling new exploits. They also noted that, in their experience, customers were happy if an exploit remained viable and zero-day for at least 12 months, though that was seen as an emotional benchmark more than based on operational data.

Implications for Defense

Defenders should live with the expectation that any zero-day vulnerabilities in their code that are particularly useful as exploits are likely deeply buried within code bases. This may mean that vendors should continually look for vulnerabilities even in areas of code they feel they have thoroughly reviewed. Having more people helping to find vulnerabilities via bug-bounty programs could help continuously bring new researchers to looking at code already deemed clean.

Finding and patching vulnerabilities in code becomes harder with software reuse between platforms and, in particular, with the Internet of Things, as more code is reused across platforms in home environments, transportation, medical systems, and beyond. The nature of Internet of Things devices often means there are no mechanisms to fix the device, and finding and patching vulnerabilities will be a challenge unless there is significant effort to maintain the infrastructure for patching.

"Software rot"—which refers to what occurs when software is not regularly updated and code is not maintained—may be a concern, as there are likely dormant vulnerabilities that will be found over time and may still be useful to exploit. As such, it may be useful to have an effort to patch zero-day vulnerabilities in no-longer-maintained software, especially for code that remains in widespread use. (Particularly for code that was produced by defunct software companies, there are no immediate options for patching or starting a bug-bounty program.) This type of effort would also be applicable for open source software.

A life expectancy of 6.9 years implies that offense may have the upper hand. As suspected, defenders likely need better tools and more options to both find zero-day vulnerabilities and detect when a system or software package is being exploited. Rather than focusing only on finding zero-day vulnerabilities or creating more tools or options to detect when a system or software package is being exploited, defenders may be able to shift the balance in their favor by starting from the assumption of compromise and investigating ways to improve system architecture design to contain the impact of compromise.

Implications for Offense

Exploit developers or those who maintain zero-days should be aware that 25 percent of their exploits will no longer be useful (as zero-days) in 1.5 years. At the same time, because the average vulnerability remains as a zero-day for almost seven years, the demand for vulnerabilities in particular software packages may decrease over time. Offensive entities may not need to stockpile for a particular software package many exploits deep, given vulnerabilities' long life; having a few vulnerabilities as backup may be sufficient. Any remaining similar vulnerabilities could be turned over to the vendor for patching, given that they would not expose the vulnerability intended to be kept operational.[1] It may be useful to develop a "cut-off radius" of proximity to the vulnerability that should remain alive.

Those who are involved with planning offensive operations using a *specific* zero-day vulnerability should consider its use only in short-term planning circumstances.

---

[1] Though, as will be discussed below, when one vulnerability is discovered and disclosed, it often leads to the discovery and disclosure of other similar vulnerabilities; this could be a factor in increasing collisions.

On the other hand, the use of *any* zero-day vulnerability may allow for a longer window of time to plan or carry out an operation.

Finding #3: No characteristics of a vulnerability indicated a long or short life; however, future analyses may want to examine Linux versus other platform types, the similarity of open and closed source code, and various groupings of exploit class type

After evaluating the vulnerability type, platform affected, source code type, and exploit class type, no characteristic statistically stood out as a "smoking gun" that might indicate a short or long life. This may have been due to either a true lack of association or a lack of statistical power to detect those associations, given the relatively small number of deaths in our dataset. The biggest obstacle was a lack of observed deaths within each characteristic level, limiting statistical power to detect differences across levels. Thus, more data may provide more statistically significant results, though whether that would confirm this finding or find that a particular characteristic *does* matter is unclear.[2]

While nothing stood out as statistically significant, our analysis *does* provide guidance on what hypotheses may be valuable to test in future analyses—in particular, to examine longevity of vulnerabilities for Linux compared with other platforms; to confirm the similarity of longevity of vulnerabilities for open and closed source code type; and to investigate any significance of grouping client-side and remote exploits together compared against a grouping of local, mixed, and other exploits.

Had any characteristics stood out statistically (which may be confirmed or refuted with more data), that may have helped those involved with vulnerability research, the vulnerabilities equities process, or the security community in general to refine decisions about which vulnerabilities should be retained and which should be publicly disclosed. If one type of vulnerability was found more often than others over a short period of time (e.g., heap overflows for OSX), perhaps that type of vulnerability should be publicly disclosed and patched (i.e., not stockpiled) because those wishing to exploit them for their own operations may have a short time to do so, and more people may be at risk given the quick discovery rate.[3] Similarly, if a particular type or aspect of a vulnerability indicates a long time, stockpiling may be a justifiable option.

---

[2]   One former manager of exploit developers surmised that there would never be a characteristic that would indicate long or short life. Rather, this individual believed that the best indicator of a long life was a vulnerability being found in a class that had already been thoroughly examined by other vulnerability researchers (e.g., font bugs). Other vulnerability researchers we spoke to agreed with this supposition.

[3]   Of course, it depends on the platform and target system affected. Even if a vulnerability is quick to develop an exploit for and has a short lifetime, a short time of using it could still prove valuable.

Implications for Defense

Security strategies must focus on all types of vulnerabilities, rather than just one kind (e.g., just memory corruption vulnerabilities, or only those in open source products). Defenders cannot focus on one particular thing to defend, since there is no characteristic that makes vulnerabilities any more or less likely.

Implications for Offense

Because there appears to be no vulnerability characteristic that indicates a shorter or longer life, it may be most efficient and cost-effective to stockpile and develop exploits for whatever vulnerabilities are easiest to find or most effective. As it stands, our data did not indicate that there are any vulnerabilities that are "stronger" or "weaker" than others in terms of resilience to being discovered and disclosed.

Finding #4: For a given stockpile of zero-day vulnerabilities, after a year, approximately 5.7 percent have been discovered and disclosed by others

The timing of "flushing" a stockpile of dead vulnerabilities matters. Collision and overlap rates changed significantly depending on the interval time used (from 40 percent to less than 1 percent).[4] We found a median value of 5.76 percent overlap (6.79 percent standard deviation) given a 365-day time interval, and a median value of 0.87 percent overlap (5.3 percent standard deviation) in the 90-day time interval. A 14-year interval (i.e., all of our data in one time interval) yielded a 40 percent overlap.

With the exception of a 14-year interval, our data show a relatively low collision rate. Some argue that this may be because those in the private exploitation and gray-market spaces look for different vulnerabilities than those hunting for vulnerabilities in the public release and white-market spaces, or that different vulnerability-finding techniques are in play, yielding different vulnerabilities found (e.g., vulnerabilities found via automatic software testing, or "fuzzing," versus vulnerabilities found via manual analysis).

We compared overlap rates between those looking for private use (the blue circle in Figure 1.2) and those looking for public release (the green circle in Figure 1.2). Those in charge of stockpiling considerations may be more interested in the overlap between two opposing groups (the blue and red circles in Figure 1.2), and this overlap may be different than what we found in our data. On the one hand, the collision rate may be

---

[4] This is a prime example of how data can be used to support a variety of viewpoints, in particular a high versus low collision rate. Those that have argued that the overlap is small (or large) do not typically specify the time interval. We have demonstrated with our data that the range can be from a fraction of a percentage to almost half—depending on the time window. Our analysis brings to light the importance of noting the time interval—otherwise, it is seemingly possible for anyone to "prove" the result they want to show, even with data.

higher, because these types of researchers may be looking for similar vulnerabilities or using similar techniques. But it may also be lower, because those in the private exploitation space tend not to stockpile deeply for the same target (i.e., as long as they have a few vulnerabilities in a given target, there is not typically a need to prioritize finding more bugs in that target). On this point, one vulnerability research team we spoke to claimed that co-discovery of their vulnerabilities happens less than once per year.

Many vulnerability researchers agree that, where one vulnerability exists, so do others. As such, once a vulnerability is found (and publicly disclosed) in one part of code, bug hunters and exploit developers tend to swarm that part of code to look for others.[5] There are some rare cases where an exploit development team has maintained capabilities in software that other heavily funded vulnerability research teams have been looking at for years.[6]

Had a significant percentage of exploits been dead, then the large overlap between what is found publicly and what is found privately might indicate an even larger overlap between what is found by disparate groups privately looking for vulnerabilities and developing exploits for their own use. As it is, the small percentage of dead exploits may indicate that those that search for vulnerabilities privately have a small overlap with each other.

Implications for Defense

Finding and crowdsourcing vulnerabilities may not be enough to secure systems, because the overlap between what is found and disclosed publicly and what is found and kept privately appears to be relatively small. This implies that vulnerabilities may either be dense or very hard to find.

The presence of *any* overlap indicates that multiple people can—and have—found same vulnerabilities in commercial products, in particular, those vulnerabilities that are valuable to nation-state type actors. As such, while approaches such as bug bounties and vulnerability detection and patching are valuable, defenders should consider employing additional efforts to create mitigations, employ better defensive measures, do more thorough (and deeper) code review before releasing a product to the public, or study the techniques of how offense finds vulnerabilities. Additionally, defenders could consider tackling software security by treating all code as insecure, and investing

---

[5]   There are many analogies for this swarm mentality of vulnerability researchers. Things we heard from people included "when you find one bug, you find others," "it's like kids' soccer—one person runs towards the ball and everyone follows," "while the ocean of bugs is deep and vast, vulnerability researchers can all smell a drop of blood in the water," and "vulturing."

[6]   While the vulnerability research and information security community is generally open and willing to share information, even hinting about vulnerability research is limited. For experienced exploit developers, someone just hinting that a bug exists in a specific library or piece of code is enough for the developers to find the bug. As such, security researchers are sometimes apt to be close-lipped about the types of vulnerabilities they have found; many believe that if they even hint or speak hypothetically about finding a vulnerability in a certain codebase, other researchers will flock to find the same or similar type of vulnerability.

efforts in careful and thorough system and network architecture design to contain the impact of eventual compromise.

Implications for Offense

Offensively focused vulnerability researchers may employ different methods of finding vulnerabilities than those who are defensively focused. Therefore, those on the offensive side may benefit by continuing to find vulnerabilities given their current techniques. This may also mean that adding vulnerability researchers to a team could help find new and unique vulnerabilities.

Though our data revealed a relatively small overlap percentage, this was only between those looking for private use and those looking for public release (i.e., the overlap between the blue and green circles in Figure 1.2), rather than two competing groups both looking for vulnerabilities for private use (i.e., blue and red circles in Figure 1.2). Our findings would be further refined with better information on how often evaluation happens (i.e., interval time used by organizations and agencies), as well as what vulnerabilities are held by other private groups.

Finding #5: Once an exploitable vulnerability has been found, time to develop a fully functioning exploit is relatively fast, with a median time of 22 days

We found that exploit development time ranges, but is generally relatively short. In our data, 71 percent of the exploits were developed in a month (31 days or less), almost a third (31.44 percent) were developed in a week or less, and only 10 percent took more than 90 days to exploit. The majority of exploits in our dataset took between 6 and 37 days to become fully functional (with a median of 22 days, minimum of 1 day, and maximum of 955 days).

The cost to develop (and, relatedly, the value or price of) an exploit can rely on many factors: the time to find a viable zero-day vulnerability (research time), the time to develop an exploit to take advantage of the zero-day vulnerability (research time), the cost of purchasing or acquiring a device or code for review, the time to set up a test lab and the cost to purchase the appropriate infrastructure or tools required for testing and analysis, the time to integrate a particular exploit into other ongoing operations, the salaries of the researchers involved in developing the exploit, the churn of the codebase—i.e., the likelihood for having to revisit the exploit and update it to new versions of the code to maintain a capability, the time a ready-to-go exploit sits unused, and supply and demand of an exploit for a particular platform or codebase. Additional value can come from a vulnerability's uniqueness (e.g., it is the only vulnerability found in a specific product) or the need and timeline of the customer.

Depending on the time it takes to find a vulnerability, and given the right talent and testing infrastructure already acquired, it may be more affordable to develop exploits in-house rather than outsource. Given accurate data on time to find a vulnerability, estimates could be made to help inform those involved with purchasing vulnerabilities of what prices they should pay for (based on labor costs alone). Certainly, the severity and impact of the vulnerability comes into play. And, while our median time to develop an exploit was 22 days, the maximum was over two and a half years, indicating that not all exploit development is the same and that it often takes very talented and dedicated researchers.

Interestingly, exploit development time does not appear to have an influence on the lifespan or survival time of an exploit.

Implications for Defense

The majority of the cost of a zero-day exploit does not come from labor, but rather the value inherent in them and the lack of supply. White-market software vendors and bug-bounty programs likely should not pay for vulnerabilities purely based on labor alone, as they do not to compete with other entities willing to buy zero-day exploits for private use.

Implications for Offense

At the most basic level, any serious attacker can always get an affordable zero-day for almost any target. However, other tangible costs (acquiring products to find the vulnerabilities in, setting up test infrastructure, maintaining and porting the exploit to work on multiple versions, renting work space, etc.) and intangible costs (premium of a high-demand, low-supply product, etc.) can cause the price to rise dramatically.

In our data, vulnerabilities purchased from external third parties had a shorter lifespan (average life of 1.4 years). This may be an argument for finding vulnerabilities and developing exploits in-house if a long life is desired.

Governments create a huge demand in this market and, for that reason, have massive buyer power. If a government coordinated its effort and used its buyer power, it could have more control over prices of exploits.

Other Recommendations for Defense

Those involved in defense may have a bigger impact on zero-day vulnerabilities than those on the offense side.

Defense may want to focus on mitigation, containment, accountability, and maintaining a robust infrastructure of patching, rather than finding and fixing vulnerabilities.[7] Mitigations (such as sandboxing and Microsoft's Enhanced Mitigation Experience Toolkit [EMET]) are seen as ways to prune out the easier-to-find vulnerabilities, but are not seen as an impossible hurdle.[8] Containment can come in the form of isolation, though it must be physical: Hypervisors and virtual isolation do not count.[9] Accountability means knowing what software is on every device, knowing what devices are present in an enterprise, and knowing what removable media has been where. This becomes a bigger challenge with the rise of the Internet of Things (see Libicki, Ablon, and Webb [2015] for more discussion).

Defense should consider strategic approaches, in addition to the more traditional tactical approaches. That is, in addition to trying to understand what exactly an exploit is doing, it may be useful to recognize that a compromise or attempt is inevitable, and aim to limit the impact of an exploit via containment and accountability.

Some believe that a government strategy should be to create new configurations and put together new workarounds that protect the public, but without releasing any information to the public about what exactly those protections are. It may be useful for the government to share more openly with the public the benefit of mitigations they are releasing, especially if they are in regard to software vulnerabilities.

Other Recommendations for Offense

Companies do not generally audit for vulnerabilities after a new code release (i.e., code refactor), but perhaps they should. While they ideally want all customers to use the newest version, this is not always reality: Some systems (e.g., ICS [industrial control system] and SCADA [supervisory control and data acquisition]) require that old versions stay in place longer than may be ideal. Other times, upgrading to the newest version or applying the latest patches means disrupting business operations and is seen as cost-prohibitive. As such, groups and organizations in the vulnerability research and exploitation development businesses should consider reexamining old code bases and previous versions—exploitable vulnerabilities may still exist, and older products may still be in use around in the world.

To beat the software testing programs ("fuzzers") and bug hunters searching for vulnerabilities in the public use space, private exploit developers may want to audit parts

---

[7] However, some companies see finding and fixing vulnerabilities as a viable strategy. For example, in February 2002, Microsoft shut down and stopped development to work on security patches for two months. See Chapter 3 of the "Security Development Lifecycle: Life in the Digital Crosshairs" on Microsoft's website (Microsoft, no date).

[8] Anti-virus solutions are not generally seen as a hurdle at all. BUSBY had seven exploits for anti-virus products: Five are still living (the oldest at 4.4 years old), and two are of uncertain life status.

[9] Five of BUSBY's exploits were for hypervisors or virtual machines. Two are dead, but one of those was intentionally killed by BUSBY.

of a code base that are most complex (or, in the words of one vulnerability researcher, "the most annoying").

Are Zero-Day Vulnerabilities Even That Big of a Deal?

Spear-phishing (i.e., sending emails that appear to be from a known or trusted sender to induce the recipient to reveal confidential information) is a major attack vector that is not typically reliant on taking advantage of vulnerabilities, zero-day or otherwise. And a majority of attacks rely on already known vulnerabilities. So it is not clear how much focus should be on zero-day vulnerabilities and their exploits: With so many instances of users not applying patches for known vulnerabilities, does it make sense to focus on the relatively few zero-day vulnerabilities?[10] Other than the few cases in which a zero-day is the only way to gain entry into a hardened target, one might infer that zero-day vulnerabilities do not matter in the grand scheme of cybersecurity. That said, there may be operations in which entry into a system or target is deemed absolutely necessary, and zero-day vulnerabilities and their exploits are the only way in.

To Stockpile or Not to Stockpile?

Governments may choose to keep zero-day vulnerabilities private, either for defensive purposes (e.g., penetration testing) or offensive operations. The decision to stockpile requires careful consideration of several factors, including the vulnerability itself, its use, the circumstances of its use, and other options that may be available to achieve an intended outcome.

Our analysis shows that zero-day vulnerabilities may have long average lifetimes and low collision rates. The small overlap may indicate that vulnerabilities are dense (i.e., another, different vulnerability usually exists) or very hard to find (with these two characteristics not necessarily mutually exclusive). If another vulnerability usually exists, then the level of protection consumers gain from a researcher disclosing a vulnerability may be seen as modest, and some may conclude that stockpiling zero-days may be a reasonable option. If zero-day vulnerabilities are very hard to find, then the small probability that others will find the same vulnerability may also support the argument to retain a stockpile.

On the other hand, our analysis shows that that the collision rates for zero-day vulnerabilities are nonzero. Some may argue that, if there is any probability that some-

---

[10] As an example, six years after the Conficker work was discovered and patched, nearly a million machines remain infected (Asghari, Cieri, and van Eeten, 2015). And past research (Libicki, Ablon, and Webb, 2015) suggests that sufficiently large organizations cannot be protected from penetration, either with zero-day or non-zero-day vulnerabilities.

one else (especially an adversary) will find the same zero-day vulnerability, then the potentially severe consequences of keeping the zero-day private and leaving a population vulnerable warrant immediate vulnerability disclosure and patch. In this line of thought, the best decision may be to stockpile *only* if one is confident that no one else will find the zero-day; disclose otherwise.

Some Caveats About Our Data

There are some caveats regarding our data, explained below.

Results from Our Data Can Be Generalized Only to Similar Datasets

Our findings are based on the dataset that we described in Chapter One. We believe these data are relatively representative of what a sophisticated nation-state might have in its arsenal. As such, a reader who is dealing with similar data could likely come to the same or similar conclusions about their data. Even so, applying wide generalizations to other datasets may be misleading, as generalizations to other data can only be drawn if the data are similar in nature to ours.[11]

"Death" Can Be a Combination of Many Things

An exploit is not necessarily just one vulnerability. A successful exploit can consist of chaining multiple vulnerabilities, so "killing" an exploit does not necessarily mean that all the vulnerabilities in the exploit were discovered. Rather, an exploit's death could be due to the discovery of just one vulnerability or component. Similarly, an exploit's resurrection could be as simple as finding a replacement for the discovered component—which may be difficult or trivial. This report focuses on exploits, rather than vulnerabilities: The life status of an exploit does not necessarily depend on the life status of the underlying vulnerability.[12]

Some Alive Exploits May Actually Be Dead

Some exploits that we categorize as alive (and unknown) may actually be dead (known to the public). If the affected vendor finds a vulnerability, it may not say as much. Furthermore, some researchers choose to not to disclose vulnerabilities they have found.

There are several reasons why an exploit developer or bug hunter may have found a vulnerability but has not disclosed it:

---

[11] This is especially true in environments experiencing rapid adoption of Internet of Things devices.

[12] For example, an exploit might exist that is a combination of a vulnerability or primitive that allows for file upload or write ability, as well as a vulnerability that allows for remote code execution. If the write primitive vulnerability is discovered, the exploit is considered to be dead even if the other vulnerability remains undetected.

- Many security researchers who work for bug-bounty or security research organizations come from organizations with an offensive or operational focus, so they recognize the importance of sitting on a vulnerability.
- Security researchers or bug hunters may have found the vulnerability with someone else (or for someone else, e.g., an offensive organization within a government agency), and if they disclose, they are giving up the capabilities of the other researcher or organization.
- It may just be the personality of the security researcher: In some exploit development circles it is considered bad form to publicly disclose them. If any sharing occurs, it may be only within certain private circles, possibly for information sharing, proof of insecurity, or pride and boasting purposes.[13]
- Security researchers may save the vulnerability for use in hacking contests that award big prize money (although there is disagreement on whether this actually happens).
- Security researchers are waiting for maintenance of a codebase to reach end of life (e.g., Windows XP) before they employ an exploit and possibly disclose.
- Some researchers may find the disclosure process with the particular vendor to be particularly challenging, so refrain from doing so.

That said, with our data, we choose to be conservative in calling vulnerabilities "alive." If anyone—intentionally or unintentionally—mentioned the vulnerability in question (even if they did not call out that it was a vulnerability), we counted it as "dead."

Other Caveats About the Data

While we spoke to others with similar data and experience developing exploits, and although we sought data from multiple sources, we received data from only one source. As such, our data are limited to the vulnerabilities from one source, and we acknowledge that they may not encompass the entire world of possibilities for exploitation.

Sometimes, participants in the software vulnerability markets specialize: One might focus on browsers and client-based software, and another might focus on web-based applications and server-side software. Others are not as discriminating.[14] Because our data came from one source, not all vulnerability or product types are represented in the data (e.g., indigenous versus commercial off-the-shelf code; server-side versus

---

[13]   For example, one exploit in our dataset characterized as living relies on a vulnerability in a class that is all but extinct (e.g., font vulnerabilities), yet it does not appear that the vulnerability has been publicly disclosed (including by researchers who have specialized in and made a living from finding those particular types of vulnerabilities, and who may have already found the vulnerability but are keeping that information private).

[14]   For more on the various markets for zero-day vulnerabilities, see Chapter Four of Libicki, Ablon, and Webb (2015).

client-side products; software versus firmware versus hardware; operating systems versus browsers).

While still an impressive amount of data entries, some may consider it small because there are only a handful of vendor, platform, and vulnerability types represented (64, 12, and 42, respectively), and some of the exploits and information had to be removed because of the sensitive nature of the work and ongoing operations. Our ability to consider multiple vulnerability characteristics simultaneously was limited, as the number of observed deaths becomes very small when cross-classifying vulnerabilities based on multiple characteristics.

Our data may also exhibit strong correlations between vulnerability characteristics.[15] For example, because most data structures and memory allocations in the Linux kernel are heap-based, memory corruption vulnerabilities in the Linux kernel tend toward heap overflows. Furthermore, because Linux is open source and Microsoft (for example) is closed source, more vulnerabilities in Linux may have a life status of Code Refactor, while more vulnerabilities in Microsoft may have an Immortal life status.

There may be historical reasons why certain vulnerabilities were found and exploited when they were. For example, long-lived vulnerabilities may only have a long life because no one is looking for them. Several years ago, people were privately and publicly looking for those vulnerabilities, but their focus may have shifted over time. This may be a reason why long-lived vulnerabilities that remained undetected will continue to go undetected, and, as such, some believe that one needs to wait through a software's full lifetime and for an entire class of vulnerabilities to be focused on, found, and mitigated in order to see what really has a long life.

Follow-On Research

This research is intended to be a starting point for research on zero-day vulnerabilities and their exploits using data and is just one tool to aid those involved in discussions. We only scratched the surface of what is possible to investigate with data. More research threads exist. For example:

- What (if any) characteristics of zero-day vulnerabilities indicate a long or short life, and what are collision rates between two similar groups? With more data, this question would be relatively trivial to explore (as our analysis mechanisms are already set up).
- Is it possible to have a reliability metric for exploits to determine the quality of the exploit?

---

[15] Some of these properties we examined within this report; others may be examined in future research.

- What overlap is there between nation-states? What are the sizes and capabilities of other nation-states?
- How do our data compare with the private vulnerability repositories of companies and of other databases?
- How does what we find compare with what our adversaries (or those who have the same motivations as us) find? Can one set of vulnerabilities (e.g., disclosed by a government or organization) help intuit what vulnerabilities might be privately held by others? How does this affect longevity or collision rates?
- What are trends over time? As we have seen, the nature of vulnerabilities is dynamic, and new mitigations can affect the longevity of exploits and shift the focus of exploit developers. If defense suddenly has the upper hand, what does that mean for the need to find vulnerabilities and create exploits from them? Should there be shifts in resource allocation?
- What is the overlap between bug bounties and those who find vulnerabilities for private exploitation? Some experts see a large overlap, while others do not (e.g., a vulnerability researcher we spoke to noted, "I have never cursed a bug bounty for foiling my plans.") What is the long-term impact of more diligent vulnerability search and testing and harnessing of bug bounties?
- What are differences in analysis after a significant amount of time (e.g., ten years from now) of similar data, and does that shed some light on whether bug-bounty programs have an impact on reducing life expectancies?
- What are the appropriate levels of liability that governments should consider? For example, if a government sat knowingly on a vulnerability that that attackers leveraged for a successful compromise against critical infrastructure or a company, should the government carry some liability?
- Are there better ways that security researchers, vendors, and governments could more proactively share information that would allow a vulnerability to be kept alive by the researchers or governments, yet still allow the affected company to better protect itself? Is there a way to provide a behavior or signature without fully exposing information about a zero-day?

The Exploit Development Cycle

The exploit development process consists of many steps, each of which can go through multiple iterations.

Phase 1: Discovery and Verification

In the first phase, vulnerability researchers search for vulnerabilities and develop a reliable proof-of-concept exploit.

Figure A.1
The Exploit Development Life Cycle

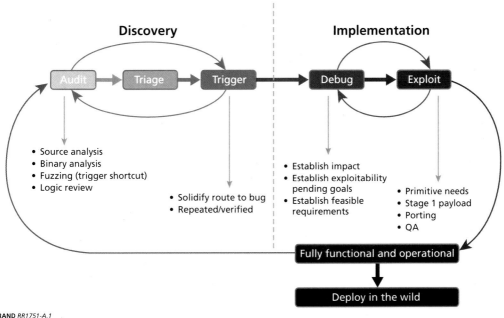

RAND *RR1751-A.1*

Step 1: Audit and Create Crashes

The first step of creating an exploit is finding a vulnerability that would be worthwhile to develop an exploit for (we call this an "exploit-worthy" vulnerability). Some error or corner case gets triggered, which causes a crash for the vulnerability researcher to investigate further.

This is code auditing, which can be fairly shallow (e.g., running an automated commercial "fuzzer" on a product[1]), or quite deep (e.g., manual static and dynamic code analysis, or taint analysis[2]). Some vulnerability research groups take pride in never using automated tools, claiming that a manual auditing strategy is one of their advantages to finding hidden vulnerabilities.

The method of finding vulnerabilities can have an impact on which vulnerabilities are actually found. As one example, recent research claims that fuzzers find only the tip of the iceberg in terms of vulnerabilities (Kirda et al., no date). Vulnerabilities can be found via fuzzing in newer or less mature products, or those with simple code bases. For products that have a longer life, are more complex, are popular with a large market share, or are high revenue generators, more people have evaluated the code bases, and finding vulnerabilities often requires more in-depth auditing, logic review, and source code analysis, in order to go several layers deep.

The probability of finding an exploit-worthy vulnerability changes depending on how many have already looked at the code, the depth of code analysis (shallow vulnerabilities are found first), the complexity of code,[3] the rate of change of the product,[4] the maturity of the product,[5] and the function of the products.[6]

Bug hunting has also become more accessible as resources (books, online guides, talks) have been made available for any interested party to be involved.

Some vulnerability researchers focus their code auditing on specific vendors,[7] while others are open to auditing a variety of products. Some, rather than focusing on

---

[1]   Not all fuzzers are created equal. Some have the ability to go deeper than others, and some find different bugs depending on their method. For example, AFL (American Fuzzy Lop) finds bugs quickly by tracking down every "if statement" in a code base.

[2]   Taint analysis follows control data put into the flow of code to see where it moves in a process. See Newsome and Song (2005) for more research using taint analysis.

[3]   The more complex the code, the more opportunities for compatibility issues and exploitable vulnerabilities.

[4]   For example, browser vendors are constantly updating and releasing new code—and thus introducing new bugs at a faster rate. In contrast, with network products, such as routers, there is a longer timetable to release new versions, feature release is longer, and the flux is low—and thus new bugs are introduced at a slower rate.

[5]   The older the product, the more likely that shallow bugs have been found. Additionally, if a product has a history of buggy code, it likely will have buggy code in the future.

[6]   Fuzzing for bugs is often faster on products that do one function and return—image readers, video parsers, music parsers, etc.

[7]   This is especially the case for companies that have in-house vulnerability research groups, where it makes most sense for them to look at their own products. One such company said that it focused on high-profile targets: products in emerging markets or with a large market share.

a specific vendor or product, search for a particular vulnerability pattern—regardless of what product it may be in.[8]

Step 2: Triage the Crashes to Determine How They Occurred

The triage process involves tracing a crash back to determine the root cause in code—that is, figuring out which piece of code caused the crash to happen. Sometimes, the piece of code turns out to be useful for manipulating more than just one crash. These pieces of code are called primitives, because they are the basic building blocks of vulnerabilities, and they can often be used in multiple exploits.[9]

Step 3: Develop a Reliable Trigger

Once it is discovered how the crash happened, the researcher needs to determine how to solidify a route to the vulnerability, and ensure that a crash can be reliably triggered as needed. It is in this stage that a PoC exploit is created.

Bug hunters, whose goal is to find vulnerabilities and share or sell that information to the affected vendor or a bug bounty program, often stop at this point.

Phase 2: Implementation

In the second phase, vulnerability researchers take their PoC exploit and create a fully functional exploit (if possible).

Step 4: Debug and Determine Requirements for Full Exploitation

Here, the vulnerability researcher evaluates the various trigger-able, reliable, crashes, to determine which is viable as a fully functional exploit (rather than just a proof of concept). Once narrowed down, the researcher determines exactly what can be done with the crash (e.g., remote code execution, information leak, crash a different process), the potential impact caused by the crash, and other requirements needed to reduce uncertainty and create a fully functional exploit (e.g., other building blocks). If other requirements are deemed necessary, the researcher may need to go back to Phase 1 to find more vulnerabilities and fill in the unknowns.

Often, an exploit will consist of multiple vulnerabilities, each contributing to the overall exploitation. For example, an exploit may require a race condition vulnerability to exist in order to then take advantage of a memory mismanagement vulnerability. Obviously, the fewer vulnerabilities needed, the easier to create a fully functioning exploit; the greater number of variables involved, the harder to exploit.

---

[8] This strategy to focus on specific patterns has potential for high reward, but also high risk: High reward because, once found, the exploit development piece is trivial, and high risk because, if the pattern is discovered by someone else, it could get patched and eliminate a researcher's capability in one fell swoop. One vulnerability researcher noted that these patterns were one of the two most important pieces of intellectual property s/he had.

[9] Examples of primitives include pieces of code that allow privilege escalation, write, read, or execute ability.

Step 5: Create Full Exploit

Once the vulnerability researcher has determined what is needed for full exploitation (i.e., come up with a theory of exploitation) and has obtained the necessary building blocks, she or he starts implementing those to fill in the unknowns. Initially, the exploit developer might focus on maintaining code execution or some initial foothold into a process (via object injection or memory corruption). Eventually, she or he would add in capabilities for continuation, port to different infrastructure and platforms,[10] create compatibility with other versions,[11] or clean up any identification of the exploit being present in the system.[12] Sometimes, exploits need to be chained together or certain operational circumstances need to be met for a desired effect to occur.[13] Now the vulnerability researcher has a fully functioning exploit.

Phase 3: Operational Handoff

Step 6: Use in the Wild

To use an exploit operationally, more steps are often taken. Use of an exploit "in the wild" may be very different than in the lab setting. In a lab, the testing environment remains the same: Network load and latency is controlled and consistent, and the system being exploited is only being used for testing purposes. Sometimes, debugging efforts in the lab introduce process behavior that would not exist in an operational environment. In an operational setting, the target system may be under heavy load, and different language packs and dynamic link libraries (dll's) may be loaded differently. Thus, any lab-based assumptions about process memory layouts may be completely invalid in an operational setting. This can significantly affect how an exploit functions.[14] As a result, success of an exploit in an operational setting can often depend on the operator's experience and training.[15]

Tool (or implant or n-stage payload) deployment is the next step—however, this is not part of the exploitation-development process.

---

[10]   Which sometimes requires going back to the initial auditing process.

[11]   For example, in Windows 2000 server, exploitation can be done remotely, but in Windows 2003 server, it is generally done locally.

[12]   For example, cleaning up memory used, if exploitation was done in kernel space.

[13]   For example, exploiting a race condition vulnerability can require positioning oneself on a target system of interest for several minutes in order to sync with multiple processes.

[14]   For example, for memory corruption exploits, successful exploitation can depend on knowing how the heap is being used, and how other system requests are being processed and handled concurrent to the exploit's system requests.

[15]   For example, recognizing that it may be necessary to deploy the exploit on a target system after hours, when network load and latency is at a minimum.

Keeping Up to Date

Exploit development is an iterative process. While not always required by customers, many exploit developers, proud of their work, will continually do audits to make sure their exploits still work when new software versions are released. This can be an exponential problem over time.

Often they are faced with an exploit that has been caught (or leaked) in the wild, and must examine whether any of the primitives used by the exploit were shared by any of their own exploits.

Only a Small Percentage of Crashes or Triggered Vulnerabilities Are Useful as Exploitable Vulnerabilities.

Despite the growing popularity of bug bounty programs and the rise of bug hunters, finding exploitable vulnerabilities in the midst of the bugs can be challenging, as only a subset of the bugs found are actually usefully exploitable. There is no blanket percentage of exploitable vulnerabilities from bugs—it depends on the vendor, product type (e.g., browsers versus routers), software development practices, etc. Some might argue that *any* crash could be considered a type of attack, and so could be useful in an operational setting, but it is generally acknowledged that only a small percentage of vulnerabilities found through auditing (manual or machine fuzzing) are actually "useful" for exploitation. Those we spoke to gave a variety of estimates for the percentage of crashes or triggered bugs that would turn into useful, exploitable vulnerabilities: 0.5–1 percent, 15–20 percent, 25–30 percent. One vulnerability researcher shared that that as high as 50 percent of vulnerabilities s/he found could be useful for exploitation, noting however, that her/his method for finding vulnerabilities reduced the number of useless vulnerabilities, and that s/he tried to exploit every vulnerability found.

Sometimes those vulnerabilities that are determined not to be exploitable are still kept on a "rainy day" shelf: If a new vulnerability researcher starts at a company, or if someone is looking for something to do, they might revisit the vulnerabilities to see whether something has changed in code to make them exploitable.

Some Factors That Can Affect Exploit Development

Mitigations Can Have a Big Impact

Mitigations affect exploitability, and can have a big impact in what gets exploited. As one might expect, security mitigations and countermeasures play a large role in the exploitability of a vulnerability. Thus, what is exploitable, and what gets exploited, can shift over time.

For example, in the past, vulnerabilities in the kernel were deemed easier to exploit than vulnerabilities in user space—largely because complexity was reduced in the kernel (e.g., null dereference).[16] As companies started to pay more attention to operating system security, new mitigations were built in, increasing the difficulty for kernel exploitation.[17]

History—Code Quality, and History of Codebase—Can Be a Good Indicator of Exploitability

History is a good indicator of exploitability. If in the past many vulnerabilities and exploits in a particular have been found in a particular code base, there is a good chance that many vulnerabilities will be found in future iterations of this code base. This may be because (1) the code base truly is riddled with vulnerabilities, and/or (2) the codebase has a large market share and has more researchers examining it and finding vulnerabilities. Researchers sometimes alert others in the information security community to code bases that have contained vulnerabilities.[18]

Tools for and Information on Exploit Development Are Widely Available, Enabling Hacking for the Masses

Resources have become more available to help formalize the vulnerability research and exploit development processes. In the 2007–2010 time frame, books, talks, classes, and online resources started to become more widely available to teach anyone how to find and exploit vulnerabilities.[19] As such, many people without a formal background started to get into exploit development.

Anyone Can Learn To Cook, but Not Everyone Can Be a Chef

Just because resources are available does not mean that anyone can write fully functional exploits. Conference talks, reports, and books can outline how an exploit was created. But taking that information and writing an exploit for a new vulnerability still requires skill. Some liken it to the culinary world: Anyone can get a recipe for a dish

---

[16] For example, in user space, one has to work with with dynamic allocations, different compiled versions, etc., whereas in the kernel, there was just one compiled distribution.

[17] Some estimates say the shift for Microsoft occurred around 2007–2008, and around 2010 (when GRSecurity was introduced) for Linux.

[18] For example, in his ZeroNights 2013 E.0x03 conference presentation, vulnerability researcher Mateusz "j00ru" Jurczyk alerts the audience that Windows kernel security vulnerabilities have been and will continue to be numerous (Jurczyk, 2013, slide 107).

[19] No Starch Press offers many books on hacking, computer security, and vulnerability research topics (No Starch Press, no date). Blogs offer insights into new techniques to exploit race conditions (e.g., StalkR, 2010). Alberts and Oldani (no date) offer an example of a conference talk discussing exploiting the Android operating system. That said, some resources were certainly around before 2007. For example, Andries Brouwer's "Hackers Hut" blog (Brouwer, 2013) has information and examples for a variety of exploitation techniques (e.g., race conditions, stack, heap).

(existing exploit) and recreate that particular dish step-by-step, but understanding how to take new ingredients (vulnerabilities) and flavor profiles (techniques) to create a new, but equally satisfying dish (new exploit) is not immediate or accessible for everyone.

Furthermore, beyond finding vulnerabilities and developing exploits, a skilled researcher also needs to know how to write good reports, to show a potential customer what the exploit is capable of.

The Human Element: Analyst Personality and Capability

The human element is a major factor in exploit development. Personality and individual capability—of the analyst auditing code, the developer writing the exploit code, and the operator employing the exploit product—influence the overall success of the final product.

Each vulnerability researcher brings her or his own skills; many become masters on a specific platform or code base, or with a certain technique (e.g., sandboxing on Windows versus Linux). Thus, changes in an exploit development team can greatly affect expected results.

Not all vulnerabilities can be equally found or exploited: The ability and personality of the vulnerability researcher matters. For example, finding and exploiting race condition vulnerabilities requires being able to visualize and keep track of multiple concurrent code paths.

Exploits with long lives (i.e., those whose vulnerabilities remain publicly unknown—and alive—for a long time) may depend on the ability of the exploit developer to go several layers deeper into code spaces than normal fuzzing (which is typically on the surface).

Some vulnerability researchers are better than others at finding exploitable vulnerabilities, and others are better at doing the exploitation. Thus, in many exploit development shops, the vulnerability researchers will pair up or work as teams.

Finally good management can vastly help a vulnerability research team succeed. Some believe that the best management has to have previous exploit development experience, in order to find the best researchers and build a good team.

The Vulnerability Researchers: Who Looks for Vulnerabilities?

Vulnerabilities would not get found (or exploited) without humans in the loop.[1] Thus, we sought to understand something about the people finding and exploiting vulnerabilities, to see how much of a role the human element plays into exploit development.

Lifetime and Seasonality of Bug Hunters and Vulnerability Researchers

In addition to information about the exploits and vulnerabilities that were exploited, our dataset contained information on the 23 vulnerability researchers that developed those exploits. Some of the researchers focused on a particular platform (e.g., specific open source platforms). Others were adept at a particular type of vulnerability (e.g., race conditions within Linux). Others were Jacks (or Jacquelines) of all trades, able to bounce between code base and vulnerability type. In our conversations with other exploit development shops, we learned that some researchers prefer to work in pairs, with one researcher preferring to do all the vulnerability finding, and the other preferring to do all the vulnerability exploitation.

Career Span of Vulnerability Researchers

Vulnerability research is a career in which many burn out (Libicki, Ablon, and Webb, 2015). Knowing the length of a viable career may be useful for planning or hiring purposes. We explore some of the characteristics of vulnerability researchers and compare this to the characteristics of those who have found publicly disclosed vulnerabilities—specifically, those of Microsoft bug hunters.

In Figure B.1, we chart out the career length of exploit developers. The start date is the first date at which the researcher recorded finding or exploiting a vulnerability (i.e., birth or mature date), and the end date is the last date that when the researcher

---

[1]   The Defense Advanced Research Projects Agency's Cyber Grand Challenge and follow-on efforts (Defense Advanced Research Projects Agency, 2016) hope to disrupt this norm, though humans are still required to code up the solutions.

Figure B.1
Length of Careers of Vulnerability Researchers While Part of BUSBY (n = 21)

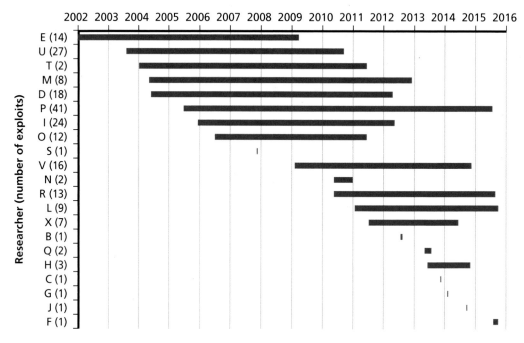

RAND RR1751-B.1

recorded finding or exploiting a vulnerability. Figure B.2 shows that the rate of development is not steady: In some years, a researcher may not find or develop an exploit.

From these data, it appears that there is a high frequency of early developers (e.g., researchers U, P, and I) versus the low frequency of later developers.[2] One might surmise that in the early years there was a lot of low-hanging fruit, or that the group of researchers peaked, lost some top performers, and is now on a downswing with less capable developers. In particular, there may be some special sauce that researchers U, P, and I have.[3]

---

[2] Due to the nature of the data (e.g., some data were removed due to operational sensitivity), these figures are incomplete, and it may appear that some of the vulnerabilities researchers (and thus the overall team) are less well-performing than was actually the case.

[3] Researcher U may have benefited from a lot of "low-hanging fruit." She or he developed her/his last exploit by 2010—around the time when many in the vulnerability researcher community agree that exploit development and mitigations for vulnerabilities started to increase dramatically and more information about vulnerability research and bug finding was publicly available, causing many vulnerabilities to be found quickly by others. Researcher P's exploits were all for Linux. As a result of this focus, s/he likely has a very deep understanding of Linux internals and kernel that enables her or him to find deeply hidden vulnerabilities. Twice as many exploits are dead as are alive for Researcher U. However, there is almost an even split between Researcher P's exploits that are still alive, and those that are dead.

Figure B.2
Years in Which Researchers Found Vulnerabilities While Part of BUSBY (n = 21)

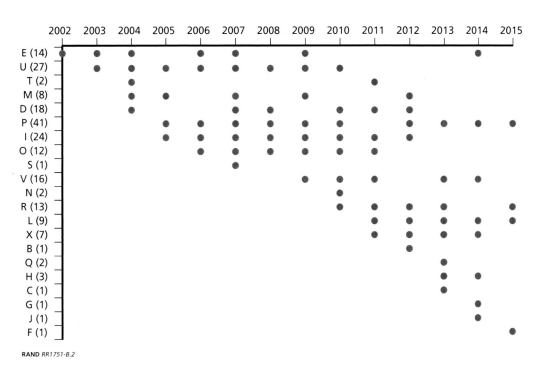

Anecdotally, another vulnerability research team noted that, for them, each researcher will ship approximately four fully working exploits per year. A developer might find more vulnerabilities and produce more proof-of-concept exploits, but many of the vulnerabilities found might not be useful for sale or not meet the requirements of the customer.[4]

Lifetime of Vulnerability Researchers in the Gray, or Government, Markets

Previous estimates had found a three-year cycle for vulnerability researchers to stay technically relevant before they start to skill out—unless they actively work to stay on top of new advances in code, mitigations, etc. (Libicki, Ablon, and Webb, 2015). While bug hunting and exploit development are different skills, we compare the length of career of vulnerability researchers in the gray, or government, markets with the lifetime of bug hunters in the white markets (i.e., bug bounties, vendors, and groups such as Google's Project Zero).

---

[4] Interestingly, white hat bug hunters who invest a great deal of time in finding vulnerabilities seem to find the same number as well. BugCrowd reported that in 2016, its top "super hunters"—those bug hunters who find the most vulnerabilities and are the most paid—submitted an average of 3.75 bugs per year (BugCrowd, 2016).

Using data from Microsoft's security advisories as a reasonable proxy for bug hunters in the white market, we calculate the average career lifetime as a bug hunter.[5] We do the same for the data we have on exploit developers, and compare. In both cases, there were hunters and researchers who found (and recorded) just one vulnerability. We compare the lifetime with and without these "one-and-done" folks. Table B.1 shows the comparison. Bug hunters who found more than one vulnerability have a recorded career length of approximately two and a half years, while exploit developers enjoy a significantly longer career length of just under four and a half years. It might be that bug hunters are jumping between products (and so their career length is underrepresented by just looking at Microsoft Security Bulletin data), or that they have other careers in the information security industry (or elsewhere) and that bug hunting is a hobby.

Table B.1
Average Recorded Career Length of Bug Hunters and BUSBY Exploit Developers

Including or Excluding "One and Done" Researchers	Bug Hunters[a]	BUSBY Exploit Developers (2002–2016)
Including	281.97 days = ~0.77 years (n = 635)	1405.28 days = ~3.85 years (n = 21)
Excluding	912.45 days = ~2.49 years (n = 284)	1639.33 days = ~4.49 years (n = 18)

[a] As recorded in Microsoft Security Bulletins, 1997–2016.

Seasonality of Vulnerability Researchers

We wanted to explore whether there was seasonality to bug hunting and vulnerability research. That is, are there certain months during the year when zero-day vulnerabilities that are worth exploiting are more or less frequently found? And are exploitable vulnerabilities found in certain months?

Defining the "birth" date as the date found by BUSBY vulnerability researchers, we separated vulnerabilities found by month (see Figure B.3).

A seasonality appears. August appears as the lowest month for finding exploitable and exploit-worthy vulnerabilities, while January appears to be the most successful month for findings vulnerabilities.[6]

---

[5]   This is likely an underrepresented sample, since some researchers may have looked for vulnerabilities in products other than Microsoft, and Microsoft may not have recorded all vulnerabilities that were reported to them. Similarly, the values for the exploit developers may also be underrepresented, since some exploits developed and vulnerabilities found were not reported or recorded in our data due to sensitivities or ongoing operational use at the time of collection.

[6]   The low count for August is statistically significant, while the high count for January is not as significant. The probability of any month having eight or fewer findings is 20 percent. The probability that it is August and there are eight or fewer vulnerabilities reported is more significant, at 2.4 percent. With 192 results, our null hypothesis

Figure B.3
Seasonality of Vulnerability Researchers: Months When Exploitable Vulnerabilities Were
Found by BUSBY Vulnerability Researchers (n = 21)

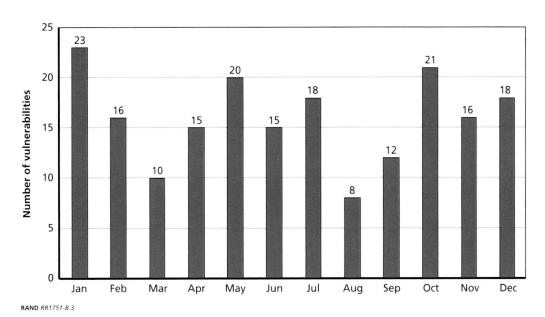

RAND RR1751-B.3

One possible explanation could be that this is a month when many of those that work for BUSBY are on summer holiday.[7] While not statistically significant, March also shows a dip. January is a big month for these bug hunters. Perhaps New Year's resolutions to find exploitable bugs contribute to the boom—or it could be that colder months mean that more people are indoors and with nothing to do but to discover exploitable vulnerabilities. March is a low month for all types of analysts: Spring break or the start of warmer weather and longer days may be a reason for the dip.

---

that each discovery happens in the month of August is probability 1/12. In this case, we would expect roughly 16 discoveries to be in August (192/12 = 16). However, there were only eight discoveries in August, which has a p-value of 0.0181. This very low p-value suggests very strong evidence that the true probability of a discovery in August is less than 1/12. Conversely, the 23 discoveries in January has a p-value of 0.05034, meaning that it is not very likely that the probability of a discovery in January is much larger than 1/12.

[7] Another explanation is that they might be attending the BlackHat and DEFCON security conferences.

How Mitigations Have Affected Exploitability: Heap Versus Stack Exploitation Case Study

Exploitability of memory corruption vulnerabilities has also shifted over time—particularly between the heap and stack. Before 2007, it was harder to exploit the heap than the stack—mostly because of differences in complexity (the stack is generally simpler to understand and manipulate than the heap).[1] Because of this, exploits based on stack overflows were more common, and, as such, security vendors focused on creating mitigations for the stack (e.g., stack cookies, stack canaries, stack address space layout randomization [ASLR]). This pushed exploit developers to focus on the heap—a harder problem at its core, but with less mitigations at the time, leading to better success once corruption paths could be figured out. By 2010, more heap protections had emerged, evening out the bias.

Although *what* got exploited (heap versus stack) changed over time, the rate of developing memory corruption vulnerabilities did not change (including time to develop an exploit), nor did it affect which vulnerabilities were discovered. Figure C.1 shows how BUSBY exploit developers shifted with developing exploits for memory corruption vulnerabilities.

---

[1] This is mostly due to the fact that the heap has multiple types of memory that can get corrupted, and it can be difficult to know which process is being affected. Even the simplest heap overflow means dealing with singly and doubly linked lists, and working with parts of code that are connected in various ways (i.e., how things are connected logically, as well as in reality). A corruption or overflow in the stack is much simpler; the stack simply goes up and down, and the algorithm to determine what memory is getting used is simpler to determine.

Figure C.1
Type of Memory Corruption, Counts by Year (n = 101)

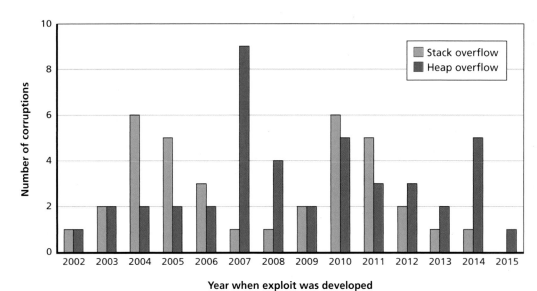

Close Collisions

A close collision is said to occur when vulnerabilities are very close to each other in code space, but only one of them is discovered, leaving the remaining vulnerability publicly unknown and able to be exploited. Sometimes, new vulnerabilities are discovered as a result of examining the code space that is disclosed in an advisory or CVE, and finding new vulnerabilities. Other times, a CVE will be released that is very close (i.e., in similar code space) to an already existing vulnerability, but the existing vulnerability still remains alive.

As one example, when it was discovered that font vulnerabilities were used in Stuxnet, many security researchers started to look for them, essentially wiping out a whole class of vulnerabilities. Some security researchers feel that, even if there are still font vulnerabilities in existence, it is not operationally worth it to find and exploit them, since so many others are looking, and the vulnerability will likely not remain publicly unknown for long.

As another example, one of BUSBY's exploits was found due to an exploit developer examining the details of a newly released vulnerability advisory, and finding other similar—and still publicly unknown (i.e., alive)—vulnerabilities.

Twenty-four of BUSBY's exploits are close collisions. As of our information cutoff date (March 1, 2016), just over a third (9) were still alive (1 is a code refactor), even though security patches and CVEs have been issued for vulnerabilities in the same code space. More than half (13) are dead (via Security Patch).[1]

Close collisions can even happen within the same company: Five of BUSBY's exploits were overlaps with others. Three were the same vulnerability, but just different algorithms, and only discovered to be the same when the CVE/advisory came out.[2] These three were all found by the same analyst (D). Two others were the same vulnerability—one for 32-bit systems and the other for 64-bit systems—and were found and exploited three years apart from each other (2005 and 2008). Those were also found by the same analyst (P).

---

[1] The remaining two are uncertain status to see whether they are still alive.

[2] Two were found and exploited within a month of each other, the third was found more than a year later.

Purchasing a Zero-Day Exploit: Some Cost and Pricing Considerations

In this appendix, we attempt to put a monetary value on finding a vulnerability and developing an exploit. We focus solely on time to find a vulnerability (research time), time to develop an exploit (exploit development time), and salary as the measure of cost. Certainly, other aspects of supply and demand can factor into the value of an exploit (as outlined in Chapter Three). As such, this analysis should be used as a starting point to refine the cost to develop an exploit.

Time to Find a Vulnerability

Time to find a vulnerability can vary based on setup, part of code examined, and age of code examined. This research time was not recorded in our data, but we spoke with six different teams, companies, or individuals who either performed or were involved with exploit development to get their first-hand input.[1] One exploit development company reported that it was very rare for their search time to exceed two months and that their average time spent looking was about a month. Another company estimated two to three weeks for audit time.

For those who create exploits, finding a vulnerability is usually done on an as-needed basis, either because a customer requested an exploit or the exploit developer needs a "place filler" (i.e., the developer had three Linux kernel vulnerabilities but two have been patched, so she or he needs to find more to have ready to go).

The longest time in the vulnerability search timeline is in the setup—for example, ensuring that a fuzzer—a code analysis tool—is tuned to the application it is testing, making sure that the file formats and architecture are correct, or getting the right configurations and infrastructure set up. For those who fuzz, once the fuzzing tool is set up, it can be very fast to find vulnerabilities—one person gave an estimate of

---

[1] This included two teams of exploit developer organizations, one group at a large commercial company that writes exploits for internal testing purposes, a former manager of a large exploit development defense contractor, a highly sought-after white hat vulnerability researcher, and a former vulnerability broker.

seconds—largely because the vulnerabilities found by fuzzers are mostly on the surface.[2] Auditing or reviewing code by hand can take much longer—days, weeks, or sometimes months—often because the researchers are going deep in the code base.

Time to find a vulnerability can depend on what part of the code is being examined,[3] what particular product is being examined, whether past tools or techniques for vulnerability detection can be used on new products,[4] and what mitigations might exist on the product.[5] The fastest-found vulnerabilities are usually in newer, smaller targets or lesser-known software, because the low-hanging vulnerabilities have not yet been found.

Often, vulnerability researchers will spend some time (estimates run from a week to a month) looking for exploitable vulnerabilities in a product; if nothing fruitful is found, they will set the project aside and come back to it later, or they may cycle it over to one of their colleagues for a fresh look. With a few exceptions,[6] this cycling might happen two or three times (maxing out at three months) before the product is put on the shelf and the researchers move onto something else.

Time to Develop an Exploit

As discussed in Chapter Three, we found that, while time to develop an exploit ranges, the majority of exploits in our dataset took between 6 and 37 days (with a median of 22 days, minimum of 1 day, and maximum of 955 days).

---

[2]   In one study, researchers found that fuzzers found less than 2 percent of bugs in a product that they injected with vulnerabilities (Kirda et al., no date, slide 24).

[3]   For example, finding a vulnerability in the kernel can often require a minimum of three to four weeks of auditing before finding an exploitable vulnerability.

[4]   For example, using the same tools or techniques across different open source browsers.

[5]   For example, Microsoft's Enhanced Mitigation Experience Toolkit (EMET) or Control Flow Guard (CFG), which make it difficult to get code running on operating systems or browsers. To bypass these types of mitigations, the exploit developers might need to use or create other exploits. This adds to the research time.

[6]   An exception is if a customer is requesting an exploit for a specific product and asks the developers to keep looking. Even then, the research is not continuous. If the exploit developers have not found anything after a few months of looking (and cycling through a handful of exploit developers), they may wait until a new version of the product comes out and spend a week looking for new vulnerabilities or code paths to previously unreachable vulnerabilities. Another exception is if the exploit developers are hired for a long-term effort on a platform (e.g., a particular type of virtual machine). They may be contracted to spend half a year looking for vulnerabilities. This type of long-term effort may result in many vulnerabilities found, only a few of which get exploited, but the rest are noted for future use if the set of vulnerabilities in the exploit get discovered and patched. Yet another example for extending the research timeline is if the product is critical to a company's business model (providing incentive for the in-house researchers to focus on it as long as possible). One group said they had been looking at a product for 18 months.

Cost Analysis: How Much Does an Exploit Cost to Develop?

Focusing solely on the cost of a developer in terms of salary, we use our estimates for time to find a vulnerability and data on time to develop an exploit to create a floor value of cost to exploit.

Base rate for exploit developer: We start with an average yearly salary of an exploit developer, X. This translates into a cost of $1.4X$ for an employer.[7] Using an average of 261 workdays in a year (U.S. Office of Personnel Management, 2016), the average daily rate of a full-time employed exploit developer is $(1.4/261)X$.

Cost to find a vulnerability: Based on the estimates received from the various exploit development companies, the range of time to find a vulnerability is two weeks to three months, with the average around a month.

Cost to develop an exploit, having found a vulnerability: Time to develop an exploit ranges, but the majority of exploits in our dataset took between 6 and 37 days (with a median of 22 days, minimum of 1 day, and maximum of 955 days).

Using $150,000 as the average salary of an exploit developer,[8] 40 percent as the overhead cost to the employer, the average time to find a vulnerability (30 days, translated into ~21.45 working days), and the median time to develop an exploit (22 days, translated into ~15.73 working days), considering only the salary of an exploit developer, an **average estimated total cost of labor per exploit is roughly $29,914.95**.

At the most basic level, it appears that any serious attacker can always get an affordable zero-day for almost any target, though other tangible costs (acquiring products to find the vulnerabilities in, setting up test infrastructure, renting work space, etc.) and intangible costs (premium of a high-demand, low-supply product, etc.) can cause the price to rise dramatically. And, to be clear, our analysis does not take into account the cost or time of failing to find vulnerabilities or to develop a fully functioning exploit. Furthermore, given the wide range of time to both find vulnerabilities and develop exploits, the true range of cost can vary widely.

Pricing to Sell

As mentioned previously, there are different efforts and levels of skill that go into finding and exploiting different vulnerabilities. Some believe that the cost of an exploit

---

[7] Estimates for additional cost of an employee to an employer range from 18 to 40 percent. (See Salary.com, 2016; Pagliery, 2013; Hadzima, 2005). We use 40 percent as a conservative estimate, especially since this just considers the obvious benefits like physical space and health insurance. There might be other benefits (such as free food or generous vacation options) that could drive it even higher.

[8] We examined job posts online for exploit developers and obtained ranges from various exploit developers and vulnerability researchers. One exploit developer also shared that junior exploit developers might make closer to $50,000 per year, and more experienced exploit developers are often in the $120,000–$140,000 range.

should increase for vulnerabilities that are more difficult to find and exploit (for example, harnessing a race condition); others believe the impact and severity of the vulnerability should be most important in determining cost.[9] Another factor is the reach and market share of the product in which the vulnerability is found.

Different markets likely have different payout schemes. Some have stated that prices in the gray (or government) and black markets are ten times those in the white market, largely because the gray and black markets are often trading in fully functional and reliable exploits, while those in the white market often just want the information about the vulnerability (Libicki, Ablon, and Webb, 2015). With a few exceptions, the white and gray markets do not intersect, mostly because there are different incentives for each.

Prices for zero-day vulnerabilities and exploits on the gray (and black) markets are hard to come by. As one broker said, "The first rule of [the] zero-days biz is to never discuss prices publicly" (quoted in Greenberg, 2015), but some limited information can be publicly found through limited publications, leaks, or, in some cases, news stories.[10] But even then, prices can vary. One vulnerability research firm we spoke to noted that their prices for exploits are three to five times those quoted in Zerodium's published price list (Zerodium, 2016).[11] Someone familiar with buying and selling zero-day vulnerabilities claimed that gray market prices of exploits for the Tor Browser Bundle were two orders of magnitude higher than prices paid on the white market for Firefox vulnerabilities. Others we spoke to noted that it is often common practice for exploit developers and brokers to exaggerate what they charge for exploits to anyone that might put it in print, in an effort to set the tone for the market. While "unicorn" exploits exist—such as iPhone full-chain exploits—they are not the norm, and rarely hit the $1 million mark. Instead, most exploits in the gray or government market are sold between $50,000–$100,000, and can go up to $150,000–$300,000, depending on the exploit. This is compared with exploits in the black market that go for less: A Flash exploit can fetch $30,000–$50,000.

Prices for zero-day vulnerabilities on the white market (e.g., bug bounties) are more readily available. Each bounty program or company has slightly different ways of formatting or presenting what they pay out, and how payouts are determined varies

---

[9]   That said, Allodi (2014) found that CVSS score may not be most indicative of use in the wild, and CVSS score or reported severity by CVE may not be accurate.

[10]   For example, Miller (2007) wrote a paper that gave some initial insights into zero-day prices. Greenberg (2012) had reported on prices for zero-day exploits, as did several news agencies. Reuters reported on the sale of a zero-day vulnerability to the FBI (Hosenball, 2016). Leaks of the Hacking Team's emails revealed prices for several zero-day vulnerabilities (Tsyrklevich, 2015). And one news article reported that the U.S. government had spent $25 million dollars in 2013 on exploits (Gellman and Nakashima, 2013).

[11]   Zerodium is a company that specializes in finding zero-day vulnerabilities and selling them to governments and corporations. Zerodium was founded by the CEO of former gray market company VUPEN, which specialized in finding zero-day vulnerabilities and selling them to government agencies.

on a number of factors. Some have published papers or articles on their particular taxonomy or method for determining payout as well as who has received how much payout.[12] Payouts for vulnerabilities average \$300–\$650 per vulnerability through bug-bounty platforms and can run into the thousands or hundreds of thousands, depending on the individual organization or company.[13]

In general, for any market, payment structure generally comes down to a few factors: how easy or hard it is to find the vulnerability (if hard, payout is greater), how many other vulnerabilities have been found in the product (if few, then vulnerabilities may be sparse, and the payout is greater), and the impact (if an exploit can go further than just remote code execution, but also bypass a mitigation, escape a sandbox, or remotely jailbreak [for mobile devices], then the payout is greater).

In the end, for those who sell their exploits, the entity that purchases the vulnerability can often be the ultimate decider of what to purchase and for how much, regardless of how long it took to find (or exploit) the vulnerability or what type of vulnerability it is.

---

[12] For example, Bugcrowd released its Defensive Vulnerability Pricing Model, where pricing for vulnerabilities is based on a number of factors, including impact of the vulnerability and security maturity of an organization (BugCrowd, 2015). Synack developed a taxonomy, where bug bounty amounts are determined by ease of discovery and threat classification (Shieber, 2014). HackerOne has published guidelines for payout of vulnerabilities for companies wishing to start their own bug bounty (HackerOne, 2016). Microsoft has an "honor roll" of bug bounty hunters (Microsoft Tech Center, 2016a).

[13] HackerOne reported that researchers using its platform earn an average of \$650 per flaw that is found (Kharpal, 2015), and BugCrowd reported that its average payout per bug was \$294.70 (BugCrowd, 2016). The U.S. Department of Defense's "Hack the Pentagon" initiative paid researchers \$100–\$15,000 (Ferdinando, 2016). Apple's bug bounty program (announced August 2016) has a maximum reward of \$200,000 (Finkle, 2016). Microsoft offered a grand prize of \$100,000 for bypass mitigation techniques (Microsoft Tech Center, 2016b).

Additional Figures and Tables

This appendix provides additional figures, tables, and charts referenced throughout this report.

Table F.1
Frequencies of Exploit-Level Characteristics Among 127 Identified Exploits

Characteristic	N (%)
Vulnerability Type	
Logic	36 (28.4%)
Memory Corruption	64 (50.4%)
Memory Mismanagement	20 (15.8%)
Mixed	6 (4.7%)
Other	1 (0.8%)
Platform Affected	
Linux	33 (26%)
Mixed	4 (3.2%)
OSX	8 (6.3%)
Open Source	13 (10.2%)
Other	3 (2.4%)
PHP	8 (6.3%)
Unix-based	10 (7.9%)
Windows	48 (37.8%)
Source Type	
Open	50 (39.4%)
Closed	70 (55.1%)
Mixed	1 (0.8%)
Unknown	6 (4.7%)
Class Type	
Client-side	12 (9.5%)
Local	50 (39.4%)
Mixed	12 (9.5%)
Other	10 (7.9%)
Remote	43 (33.9%)

Table F.2 provides the number of exploits still living at the beginning of one-year intervals, the number observed to die, and the number lost to follow up due to censoring (i.e., at the end of our sample time of 2002–2016, these were vulnerabilities that were still alive, but we could not say anything about their survival probability).

Table F.2
Life Table, All Data

Interval Start Year	Interval End Year	Beginning Total	Deaths	Censored	Survival Probability (95% CI)
0	1	127	26	5	0.79 (0.71, 0.85)
1	2	96	10	7	0.71 (0.62, 0.78)
2	3	79	8	9	0.63 (0.54, 0.71)
3	4	62	5	7	0.58 (0.48, 0.66)
4	5	50	6	10	0.50 (0.40, 0.59)
5	6	34	3	10	0.45 (0.34, 0.55)
6	7	21	1	3	0.42 (0.32, 0.53)
7	8	17	3	7	0.33 (0.21, 0.46)
8	9	7	0	4	0.33 (0.21, 0.46)
9	10	3	1	1	0.20 (0.04, 0.44)
10	11	1	0	1	0.20 (0.04, 0.44)

Figure F.1 shows the exponential, Weibull, and log-normal survival models for their fit to our data by comparing their estimated survival plots to the Kaplan-Meier plots. All three parametric models lie within the confidence band around the Kaplan-Meier curve, though they tend to overestimate the Kaplan-Meier curve in the first two years. Subsequently, each approximates the Kaplan-Meier curve's general shape, with differing rates of decay starting in year five. We chose the exponential model, shown in red. We used the decay parameter from the exponential model to plot exponential survival curves (i.e., where the curve eventually reaches or gets very close to zero survivability—something that we could not do with the data alone) along with 95 percent confidence intervals of the overall data, as well as by specific exploit characteristics.

Figure F.2 shows the smoothed hazard function corresponding to the life table plot. Higher values indicate where danger of death is highest.

The pointwise 95 percent confidence band is included to help put these bumps and dips into perspective: As shown in Figure F.2, the confidence band is generally wide relative to the sizes of the bumps and dips, which indicates that the hazard is fairly constant over time, and there is not strong evidence that any particular number

Figure F.1
Comparing Parametric Models to Kaplan-Meier (n = 127)

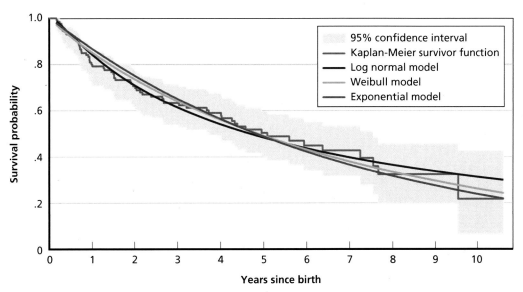

RAND *RR1751-F.1*

Figure F.2
Smoothed Hazard Function

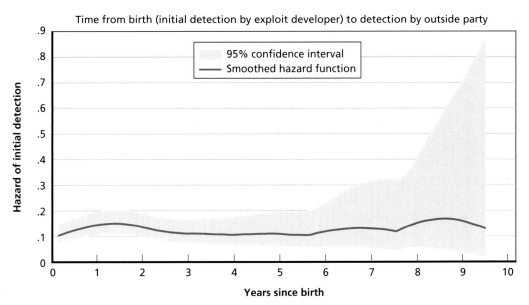

RAND *RR1751-F.2*

or years since birth is more hazardous for death than others. The further out in time we look, the wider the confidence band and the less certain we become of the true shape of that hazard function. That the hazard is approximately constant is good justification for our use of the exponential survival model for estimating life expectancy, as the exponential model is built on the assumption of a constant hazard. In our case, that hazard value is 0.145 (95 percent confidence interval: 0.113, 0.186), which visually is right along that horizontal corridor in Figure F.2. It is this hazard value of 0.145, along with its own confidence bounds, that we have used to generate the exponential model-based estimates of expected lifetime.

We used Cox proportional hazards regression modeling to determine the hazard ratio for each characteristic.

The hazard function itself can be interpreted as the instantaneous probability of death at any given time t, assuming a vulnerability had gone undetected up to that point in time. The hazard ratio associated with a given characteristic is the fraction formed by dividing the hazard for one group at time t by that of a comparison (or referent) group at the same moment. It is similar in concept to a relative risk, where a large number indicates more danger of an event compared with the referent group, and a lower number indicates less. A hazard ratio of one indicates that members of both groups are equally likely to fail at any given time. For example, if the hazard of failure at two years for memory corruption is 0.14, and the hazard of failure for memory mismanagement vulnerabilities is 0.11, then the ratio of these two is the hazard ratio of 1.27. Moreover, with a Cox proportional hazards model, we assume that this relationship between the hazard functions is constant over time; the hazard of failure may rise and fall for both of these types of vulnerabilities, but that the ratio between them is constant over time. The hazard of failure for memory corruption vulnerabilities is always 1.27 times greater than that of the memory mismanagement vulnerabilities. The modeling procedure also allows us to test this ratio for statistical significance, where we compare it to a null hypothesis value of 1.0, meaning that the hazard functions are always equal.

For each characteristic, we chose one category to be the referent category, whose hazard function would serve as the denominator in hazard ratios like the one described above.[1] Three different models were calculated to obtain:

1. unadjusted hazard ratio
2. fully adjusted hazard ratio
3. partially adjusted hazard ratio.

---

[1]   It is often advantageous to choose a referent group that has a large number of records, so you get as much power as possible for the tests of each of the individual hazard ratio (against the null hypothesis value of 1, which means the hazards are equal). From a scientific standpoint though, one can also choose the type that is considered the "most normal" to more easily comprehend estimates that are relative to that type. We chose a combination of both (large number of records and "most normal").

In the unadjusted model, each characteristic (vulnerability type, platform affected, source type, class type) was evaluated separately, to see whether any property within those characteristics indicates a long or short life. The p-values found here appeared on the graphs in Figure 3.7.[2] In the fully adjusted model, each characteristic is adjusted for simultaneously in a common model. In the partially adjusted model, we removed the "platform affected" category, because source type is heavily correlated to the platform affected (e.g., all Windows is closed source) and just performed regression adjusting for vulnerability type, source type, and class type. The higher the hazard ratio, the higher hazard of death, or higher probability of being detected, compared with the reference category. For example, examining exploit class type, at any given time that the exploits are still alive and publicly unknown, a client-side exploit is 1.02 times more likely to die than a remote exploit, whereas a local exploit is 72 percent as likely to be detected, for any moment in time.

Table F.3 shows the hazard ratio for each characteristic. In all three hazard ratio estimates, the p-values are too large to draw any concrete conclusions or indicate that these results are statistically significant. Correspondingly large confidence intervals around each estimate include the null hypothesis value of one, which as the p-values also indicate, tell us that we cannot rule out the null hypothesis value of 1 in any of the hazard ratio estimates.

---

[2] A low p-value (i.e., 0.1 or smaller) would indicate that the results are statistically significant. Given the high p-values, we are unable to infer any meaningful associations between exploit characteristics and the risk of death.

Table F.3
Hazard Ratio Estimates Obtained from Cox Proportional Hazards Modeling, with and Without Adjustment for Characteristics as Shown

Exploit Characteristics	Unadjusted Hazard Ratio (separate models)	P-Value	Fully Adjusted Hazard Ratio	P-Value	Partially Adjusted Hazard Ratio	P-Value
Vulnerability Type		0.646		0.518		0.458
Logic	1.17 (0.50, 2.75)	0.715	0.91 (0.36, 2.34)	0.846	0.87 (0.36, 2.11)	0.757
Memory Corruption	1.27 (0.59, 2.74)	0.549	0.84 (0.34, 2.05)	0.697	0.83 (0.35, 1.98)	0.680
Memory Mismanagement	1 (referent)	-	1 (referent)	-	1 (referent)	-
Mixed or Other	2.12 (0.69, 6.53)	0.191	2.04 (0.59, 7.09)	0.264	1.88 (0.61, 5.84)	0.273
Platform Affected		0.991		0.688		
Linux	0.78 (0.41, 1.48)	0.447	0.48 (0.18, 1.30)	0.149		
Mixed	0.89 (0.12, 6.58)	0.905	1.44 (0.18, 11.31)	0.728		
OSX	1.26 (0.44, 3.65)	0.668	1.30 (0.41, 4.12)	0.652		
Open Source	0.92 (0.40, 2.14)	0.845	0.53 (0.18, 1.59)	0.259		
Other	1.15 (0.27, 4.91)	0.853	0.60 (0.11, 3.17)	0.549		
PHP	1.09 (0.33, 3.62)	0.892	1.60 (0.24, 10.72)	0.626		
Unix-based	1.07 (0.41, 2.83)	0.887	0.61 (0.19, 1.97)	0.412		
Windows	1 (referent)	-	1 (referent)	-		
Source Type[a]		0.732		0.148		0.469
Open	1.09 (0.66, 1.82)	0.732	1.93 (0.79, 4.67)	0.148	1.24 (0.70, 2.19)	0.469
Closed	1 (referent)	-	1 (referent)	-	1 (referent)	-
Class Type		0.224		0.224		0.239
Client-side	1.02 (0.46, 2.27)	0.969	0.93 (0.40, 2.20)	0.872	1.04 (0.46, 2.37)	0.925
Local	0.72 (0.41, 1.27)	0.255	0.62 (0.30, 1.32)	0.214	0.60 (0.31, 1.17)	0.134
Mixed	0.64 (0.25, 1.69)	0.373	0.65 (0.24, 1.78)	0.406	0.61 (0.23, 1.62)	0.318
Other	0.26 (0.06, 1.12)	0.071	0.15 (0.03, 0.83)	0.030	0.23 (0.05, 1.04)	0.057
Remote	1 (referent)	-	1 (referent)	-	1 (referent)	-

[a] One exploit of mixed source type and six of unknown source types were excluded from analysis.

Table F.4
Vulnerability Types by Time Interval, Percentages (n = 192)

Life Status	365-Day Interval (median, std deviation)	90-Day Interval (median, std deviation)	30-Day Interval (median, std deviation)
Expanded Groups			
Immortal	11.54 (22.2)	12.79 (26.3)	12.79 (26.79)
Living	47.745 (13.98)	49.38 (16.48)	48.84 (16.56)
Undisclosed Code Refactor	4.23 (6.85)	4.9 (8.19)	4.72 (8.66)
Disclosed Code Refactor	11.52 (5.33)	10.43 (5.54)	11.01 (5.63)
Security Patch	4.52 (5.28)	0.85 (3.3)	0 (2.02)
Public Disclosure	0 (0.52)	0 (0.26)	0 (0.16)
Killed by BUSBY	0 (4.24)	0 (3.59	0 (2.05)
Unknown	17.49 (6.71)	18.6 (7.47)	18.8 (7.62)
Collapsed Groups			
Living	66.86 (11.48)	69.11 (11.37)	69.45 (11.87)
Dead in this window	5.765 (6.79)	0.87 (5.3)	0 (3.05)
Disclosed Code Refactor	11.52 (5.33)	10.43 (5.54)	11.01 (5.63)
Unknown	17.49 (6.71)	18.6 (7.47)	18.8 (7.62)

Figure F.3
365-Day Time Interval, with Percentages per Group and Interval

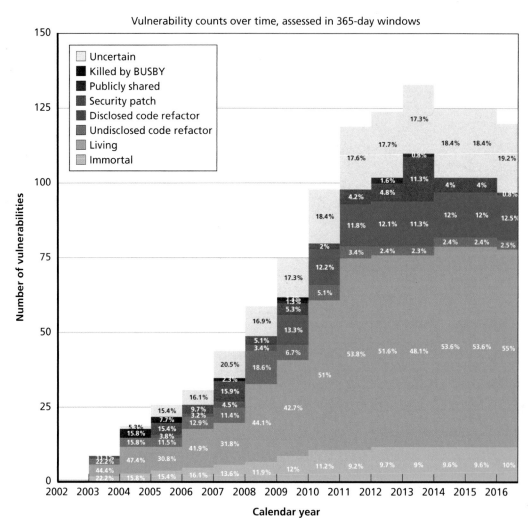

More Information About the Data

Our data spans many categories. Below are frequency counts for our data, to provide a sense of the richness and breadth of information.

Due to sensitivities, we do not include a table of all vendors that were affected, and instead provide the following summary: This dataset includes exploits for 64 vendors, with a range of 1 to 55 exploits per vendor. Microsoft (n = 55), Linux (n = 39), Apple (n = 14), and SUN/Oracle (n = 11) each had the most number of exploits, while the majority of the other vendors each had one or two exploits. These include well-known vendors such as Mozilla, LinkSys, Google, Citrix, AOL, Ethereal, Adobe, Alt-N Technologies, CryptoCat, and RealPlayer/RealServer, as well as some lesser-known vendors.

Table G.1
Data Frequency Counts

Row Labels	Count
Life Status	
Living	66
Code Refactor	21
Immortal	13
Killed by BUSBY	8
Other—feature not patchable; no longer relevant; relocated to different part of code	3
Public Disclosure/Made Public	6
Security Patch	69
Team Check	16
Unknown	5
Total	207
Vulnerability Type (high level)	
Hidden features	1
Logic	57

Table G.1—continued

Row Labels	Count
Logic, cryptographic	1
Logic; memory mismanagement	7
Logic; memory mismanagement; memory corruption	2
Memory corruption	106
Memory corruption; memory mismanagement	2
Memory mismanagement	29
Memory mismanagement; denial of service	1
Undetermined (crash)	1
Total	207
Vulnerability Type (low level)	
Allows you to remap memory in way you shouldn't	1
API misuse	3
Arbitrary free	1
Association context	1
Authentication bypass	5
Auto execution	1
BSS Overflow (like a Stack Overflow)	1
Bypass	1
Call-gate mismanagement—not checking parameters	2
Command Injection	3
Context swap; stack misalignment	1
Data overflow	1
Design misuse	1
Directory traversal; input validation	1
DNS cache poisoning	1
Environment Insertion (can insert other programs to execute)	1
Executable file upload	1
Fault handling (CPU)	1
File normalization error (interpretation of values different on different platforms)	1
File read prim (i.e., can read any file on the system)	1
File read prim (i.e., can read any file on the system); SQLi; path injection	1
Heap overflow	58

Table G.1—continued

Row Labels	Count
Heap overflow (as a result of integer overflow)	1
Hypervisor integrity issue	1
Information disclosure; kernel mismanagement	1
Information leak	3
Information leak; heap overflow	1
Integer mismanagement	1
Integer overflow	2
Integer truncation (so can be either heap or stack overflow)	1
Invalid pointer dereference	1
IO control based on write primitives	1
IPC integrity (interprocess communication)	1
Keyspace reduction	1
Leads to info leak	1
Left hardcoded admin password	1
Logic (race condition) that triggers memory corruption	1
Name validation	1
Null dereference	12
Object injection/ deserialization	4
Out of bounds write	1
Permissions on kernel device	1
Privilege escalation	2
Privilege file read	1
Privilege mismanagement	2
Privilege spoofing	1
Race condition	16
Race condition that leads to invalid pointer dereference	1
Race condition; allows you to manipulate memory	1
Race condition; out of bounds read; heap overflow	1
Race condition; use after free	1
Reference condition	2
Reference condition—that leads to object mismanagement	1
Reference condition overwrap	1
Register/memory mismanagement	1

Table G.1—continued

Row Labels	Count
Remote code injection	1
SQLi	1
Stack overflow	40
Stack overflow (x2); memory	1
Stack overflow; heap overflow	1
Type confusion/object mismanagement	1
Unsecure environment variables (so can eventually take advantage of protected environment variables)	1
Use after free	2
Uses unverified supply pointer value (blindly follows a pointer)	2
XSS	1
Total	207
Exploit Class	
Bypass	1
Client-side	25
Client-side, remote	3
Client-side, remote, denial of service	1
Context dependent	8
Crypto	1
Denial of service	3
Infoleak	3
Local	76
Local, remote	5
Local, sandbox escape	1
Network	1
Physical access hardware	1
Remote	71
Sandbox/Hypervisor Escape	6
SQLi	1
Total	207
Platform Affected	
Android	3
Embedded	1
FreeBSD	3

Table G.1—continued

Row Labels	Count
Java	1
JavaScript	1
Linux	56
N/A	3
Open source	16
OSX	18
PHP	11
Solaris	9
UNIX	2
Windows	93
Total[a]	217
Source Code Type	
No information available	8
Closed	123
Mix	2
Open	74
Total	207

[a] Some exploits work on multiple platforms. For 10 exploits, 2 or more platforms were affected.

Glossary

In the list below, we provide a list of terms and definitions to supplement the reader's understanding of software vulnerabilities and exploits. We include in this list the vulnerability types and exploit types that we used to categorize the exploits in our dataset, as described in Chapter Three.

As mentioned in Chapter Three, vulnerability types are not mutually exclusive and often become intertwined, or even interdependent, especially when considering full exploit chains, which often rely on a variety of vulnerability primitives spanning multiple classifications. A web application attack that initially relies on a logic vulnerability might trigger a memory corruption or inject objects into the underlying framework process memory space. Furthermore, "logic" as a vulnerability type is very broad and could be segmented into several other categories. A logic flaw, such as a race condition, may result in low-level issues, such as memory corruption, and memory mismanagement, but it may also result in higher-level issues, such as database query injection. Generally speaking, however, one can distinguish between low-level memory vulnerabilities that are process-critical (i.e., they crash a process) and high-level logic vulnerabilities that allow an attacker to influence program behavior but that do not necessarily risk underlying process availability.

Alive (zero-day classification)	Publicly unknown vulnerability.
black market	The trade or traffic of hacking tools, hacking services, and the fruits of hacking for malicious intent. Vulnerabilities are sold for criminal use or illicit purposes and remain private.
buffer overflow	A condition that occurs when a program attempts to put more data in a buffer than it can hold or when a program attempts to put data in a memory area past a buffer (Open Web Application Security Project [OWASP], undated-a).
bug	Software flaw.

bug bounty	A program established to provide a reward for finding and reporting a bug or vulnerability in a particular computer software product (Techopedia, undated). May also refer to the reward itself.
client-side (exploit class type)	A type of local exploit that requires human interaction to complete an action.
code churn	Code that gets updated (or refactored) to new versions. Vulnerabilities may still be present in past versions. Similar to *Code Refactor*.
Code Refactor (zero-day classification)	A likely publicly unknown vulnerability for past versions of a product that is no longer exploitable in current versions due to code revisions; the product is still maintained (so a security patch sometime in the future is still possible for the past versions). Such zero-days are also known as *zombies*.
collision, collision rate	A *collision* occurs when a two (or more) researchers independently find the same vulnerability. The collision rate is the likelihood of this happening. The *collision rate* is sometimes also referred to as the *overlap rate*.
Common Vulnerabilities and Exposures	A dictionary of common names (i.e., CVE Identifiers) for publicly known cybersecurity vulnerabilities (MITRE, undated).
Dead (zero-day classification)	Publicly known vulnerability.
denial of service	An attack focused on making a resource (site, application, server) unavailable for the purpose it was designed (OWASP, undated-b).
exploit	Malicious code that takes advantage of software vulnerabilities to infect, disrupt, or take control of a computer without the user's consent and typically without their knowledge (Microsoft, 2013). An exploit provides initial access and often the ability for code execution by taking advantage of some vulnerability in a system process, and then facilitates an implant or implant's payload.
fuzzing, fuzzer	*Fuzzing* refers to automatic software testing, usually to find vulnerabilities. A *fuzzer* is a program that performs such testing.

government market	See *gray market*.
gray market	A market for vulnerabilities in which vulnerabilities remain private, are used for either offensive or defensive purposes, and may eventually get disclosed to the affected vendor, though that is not guaranteed because they are typically first sold to a government, military, or defense contractor. The gray market is also referred to as the *government market*.
heap	An area of pre-reserved computer main storage (memory) that a program process can use to store data in some variable amount that won't be known until the program is running (Techtarget, undated-a).
Immortal (zero-day classification)	A publicly unknown vulnerability for the version of the product it was created for; that product is no longer maintained (so a security patch will never be issued).
implant	A program that solidifies and maintains access initially provided by an exploit (i.e., achieves persistence) and delivers some effect to the system.
kernel	A program that constitutes the central core of a computer operating system. It has complete control over everything that occurs in the system (linfo, undated).
Living (zero-day classification)	A publicly unknown vulnerability for current versions of the product; not found and publicly noted by anyone else (as far as it is known); those in defensive roles are likely actively looking for it.
local (exploit class type)	An exploit that requires prior access to a vulnerable system (e.g., privilege escalation)
logic (vulnerability type)	Vulnerabilities for which the base primitive is based on a flaw in higher-level program logic (e.g., race conditions).
memory corruption (vulnerability type)	Vulnerabilities for which the base primitive is based on low-level corruption of process memory (e.g., buffer overflow).
memory mismanagement (vulnerability type)	Vulnerabilities for which the base primitive is based on low-level mismanagement of process memory (e.g., use after free).

overlap, overlap rate	When a two (or more) researchers independently find the same vulnerability, the vulnerability is said to have *overlap*. The *overlap rate*, also known as the *collision rate*, is the likelihood that a vulnerability has overlap.
penetration testing	A test to determine how a system reacts to an attack, whether or not a system's defenses can be breached, and what information can be acquired from the system (Krutz and Vines, 2006).
primitive	The basic building blocks of vulnerabilities, which can often be used in multiple exploits.
proof of concept (PoC)	A demonstration that a fully functional exploit is possible on a target system. However, a PoC does not include final steps to make the exploit weaponized (this is done by clients armed with specifications about a target environment and containing the necessary obfuscation or evasion capabilities). One PoC test is the ability to cause the calculator program (calc.exe) to open up on a desktop (the "pop calc" test).
remote (exploit class type)	An exploit that does not require prior access to a vulnerable system. A remote exploit may or may not allow an operator to perform additional tasks, as the system that the attacker gets onto may have low-level privileges. Often, a successful operation requires a combination of a local or client-side exploit and remote exploit.
remote code execution	The ability to trigger arbitrary code execution from one machine on another (Wikipedia, undated-a).
sandbox, sandboxing	A tightly controlled environment that restricts permissions on what can be run (to prevent malicious code from executing or accessing something it should not, for example).
sandbox escape	Code that can escape a sandbox.
stack	A data area or buffer used for storing requests that need to be handled (Techtarget, undated-b).
vulnerability	A software, hardware, procedural, or human weakness that may provide an attacker with an open door with which to exploit. A type of bug that creates a security weakness in the design, implementation, or operation of a system or application (NRC, 1999).

white market   A market for vulnerabilities in which the vulnerabilities are
                          returned immediately to the affected vendor (often moving
                          them into the public knowledge space), for defensive pur-
                          poses. Includes bug-bounty programs, vendors, vulnerability
                          feeds, and groups such as Google's Project Zero.

zero-day vulnerability   Exploitable vulnerabilities that a software vendor is unaware
                          of and for which no patch or fix has been publicly released.

zombie   See *Code Refactor.*

References

Ablon, Lillian, Martin C. Libicki, and Andrea A. Golay, *Markets for Cybercrime Tools and Stolen Data: Hackers' Bazaar,* Santa Monica, Calif.: RAND Corporation, RR-610-JNI, 2014. As of January 30, 2017:
http://www.rand.org/pubs/research_reports/RR610.html

Alberts, Bas, and Massimiliano Oldani, "Beating up on Android—Practical Android Attacks," Immunity Inc., no date. As of 2011:
http://archives.scovetta.com/pub/conferences/infiltrate_2011/Android_Attacks.odt.pdf

Allodi, Luca, and Fabio Massacci, "Comparing Vulnerability Severity and Exploits Using Case-Control Studies," ACM Transactions on Information and System Security (TISSEC), Vol. 17, No. 1, Article 1, August 2014. As of January 30, 2017:
http://disi.unitn.it/~allodi/allodi-tissec-14.pdf

Altinkemer, Kemal, Jackie Rees, and Sanjay Sridhar, "Vulnerabilities and Patches of Open Source Software: An Empirical Study," *Journal of Information System Security*, Vol. 4, No. 2, 2008, pp. 3–25.

Asghari, Hadi, Michael Ciere, and Michel J. G. van Eeten, "Post-Mortem of a Zombie: Conficker Cleanup After Six Years," paper presented at the 24th USENIX Security Symposium, Washington, D.C., August 12–14, 2015. As of January 30, 2017:
https://www.usenix.org/system/files/conference/usenixsecurity15/sec15-paper-asghari.pdf

Bilge, Leyla, and Tudor Dumitras, "Before We Knew It: An Empirical Study of Zero-Day Attacks in the Real World," in *Proceedings of the 2012 ACM Conference on Computer and Communications Security*, New York: ACM, 2012. As of January 30, 2017:
https://users.ece.cmu.edu/~tdumitra/public_documents/bilge12_zero_day.pdf

Bland, J. Martin, "Survival Probabilities (the Kaplan-Meier Method)," *BMJ*, December 5, 1998.

Brouwer, Andries, "Hackers Hut," 2013. As of January 30, 2017:
https://www.win.tue.nl/~aeb/linux/hh/hh.html#toc9

BugCrowd, "What's a Bug Worth?" 2015. As of January 30, 2017:
https://pages.bugcrowd.com/whats-a-bug-worth-2015

———, "The State of Bug Bounty," June 2016. As of January 30, 2017:
https://pages.bugcrowd.com/hubfs/PDFs/state-of-bug-bounty-2016.pdf

Clark, Sandy, Stefan Frei, Matt Blaze, and Jonathan Smith, "Familiarity Breeds Contempt: The Honeymoon Effect and the Role of Legacy Code in Zero-Day Vulnerabilities," in *Proceedings of the 26th Annual Computer Security Applications Conference*, New York: ACM, 2010, pp. 251–260.

Clarke, Richard A., Michael J. Morell, Geoffrey R. Stone, Cass R. Sunstein, and Peter Swire, *Liberty and Security in a Changing World: Report and Recommendations of the President's Review Group on Intelligence and Communications Technologies*, December 12, 2013. As of February 6, 2017:
https://www.justsecurity.org/wp-content/uploads/2013/12/2013-12-12_rg_final_report.pdf

Crocker, Andrew, "What to Do About Lawless Government Hacking and the Weakening of Digital Security," Electronic Frontier Foundation, August 1, 2016. As of January 30, 2017:
https://www.eff.org/deeplinks/2016/08/what-do-about-lawless-government-hacking-and-weakening-digital-security

Dai Zovi, Dino, Twitter post, August 1, 2016,
https://twitter.com/dinodaizovi/status/766744230471540742

Daniel, Michael, "Heartbleed: Understanding When We Disclose Cyber Vulnerabilities," White House archives, April 28, 2014. As of January 30, 2017:
https://obamawhitehouse.archives.gov/blog/2014/04/28/
heartbleed-understanding-when-we-disclose-cyber-vulnerabilities

Defense Advanced Research Projects Agency, Cyber Grand Challenge Competitor Portal, website, 2016: As of January 30, 2017:
https://cgc.darpa.mil/

Exodus Intelligence, "Changing to Coordinated Disclosure," May 17, 2016. As of January 30, 2017:
https://blog.exodusintel.com/2016/02/18/changing-to-coordinated-disclosure/

Ferdinando, Lisa, "Carter Announces 'Hack the Pentagon' Program Results," U.S. Department of Defense, June 17, 2016. As of January 30, 2017:
http://www.defense.gov/News/Article/Article/802828/
carter-announces-hack-the-pentagon-program-results

Fidler, Mailyn, Jennifer Granick, and Martha Crenshaw, *Anarchy or Regulation: Controlling the Global Trade in Zero-Day Vulnerabilities*, master's thesis, Stanford University, 2014. As of January 30, 2017:
https://stacks.stanford.edu/file/druid:zs241cm7504/Zero-Day%20Vulnerability%20Thesis%20
by%20Fidler.pdf

Finifter, Matthew, Devdatta Akhawe, and David Wagner, "An Empirical Study of Vulnerability Rewards Programs." *USENIX Security*, Vol. 13, 2013. As of January 30, 2017:
https://www.cs.berkeley.edu/~daw/papers/vrp-use13.pdf

Finkle, Jim, "Apple Offers Big Cash Rewards for Help Finding Security Bugs," Reuters, August 5, 2016. As of January 30, 2017:
http://www.reuters.com/article/us-cyber-blackhat-apple-idUSKCN10F2TX

Geer, Dan, "Cybersecurity as Realpolitik," BlackHat, August 6, 2014. As of January 30, 2017:
http://geer.tinho.net/geer.blackhat.6viii14.txt

Gellman, Barton, and Ellen Nakashima, "U.S. Spy Agencies Mounted 231 Offensive Cyber-Operations in 2011, Documents Show," *Washington Post*, August 30, 2013. As of January 30, 2017:
https://www.washingtonpost.com/world/national-security/us-spy-agencies-mounted-231-offensive-cyber-operations-in-2011-documents-show/2013/08/30/d090a6ae-119e-11e3-b4cb-fd7ce041d814_story.html

Goel, Manish Kumar, Pardeep Khanna, and Jugal Kishore, "Understanding Survival Analysis: Kaplan-Meier Estimate," International Journal of Ayurveda Research, Vol. 1., No. 4, October–December 2010, pp. 274–278.

Greenberg, Andy, "Shopping for Zero-Days: A Price List for Hackers' Secret Software Exploits," Forbes.com, March 23, 2012. As of January 30, 2017:
http://www.forbes.com/sites/andygreenberg/2012/03/23/
shopping-for-zero-days-an-price-list-for-hackers-secret-software-exploits/

———, "Here's a Spy Firm's Price List for Secret Hacker Techniques," *Wired*, November 11, 2015. As of January 30, 2017:
https://www.wired.com/2015/11/heres-a-spy-firms-price-list-for-secret-hacker-techniques/

HackerOne, "How Should We Price Bounties?" 2016. As of September 14, 2016:
https://support.hackerone.com/hc/en-us/articles/204950689-How-should-we-price-bounties-

Hadzima, Joe, "How Much Does an Employee Cost?" *Boston Business Journal*, 2005. As of January 30, 2017:
http://web.mit.edu/e-club/hadzima/how-much-does-an-employee-cost.html

hdmoore, "Security Flaws in Universal Plug and Play: Unplug, Don't Play," Rapid7Community, January 29, 2013. As of January 30, 2017:
https://community.rapid7.com/community/infosec/blog/2013/01/29/
security-flaws-in-universal-plug-and-play-unplug-dont-play

Hosenball, Mark, "FBI Paid Under $1 Million to Unlock San Bernardino iPhone: Sources," Reuters, May 4, 2016. As of January 30, 2017:
http://www.reuters.com/article/us-apple-encryption-idUSKCN0XQ032

Jurczyk, Mateuz, "Windows Kernel Trap Handler and NTVDM Vulnerabilities—Case Study," 2013. As of September 14, 2016:
http://www.slideshare.net/DefconRussia/
mateusz-j00ru-jurczyk-windows-kernel-trap-handler-and-ntvdm-vulnerabilities-case-study

Kharpal, Arjun, "Ethical Hacking: Are Companies Ready?" CNBC, June 17, 2015. As of January 30, 2017:
http://www.cnbc.com/2015/06/17/are-companies-still-scared-of-white-hat-hackers.html

Kirda, Engin, Andrea Mambretti, Wil Robertson, Brendan Dolan-Gavitt, Patrick Hulin, and Frederich Ulrich, "LAVA: Large-scale Automated Vulnerability Addition," presentation, New York University, no date. As of January 30, 2017:
http://panda.moyix.net/~moyix/LAVA_Sapienza.pdf

Krutz, Ronald L., and Russell Dean Vines, *The CISSP® and CAPCM Prep Guide: Platinum Edition*, New York: John Wiley & Sons, 2006.

Kuehn, Andreas, and Milton Mueller, "Analyzing Bug Bounty Programs: An Institutional Perspective on the Economics of Software Vulnerabilities," paper presented at 2014 TPRC: The 42nd Research Conference on Communication, Information and Internet Policy, August 1, 2014.

Lam, Mimi, presentation explaining the purpose of the Kaplan-Meier estimator, Vanderbilt University, Department of Biostatistics wiki, no date. As of January 30, 2017:
http://biostat.mc.vanderbilt.edu/wiki/pub/Main/ClinStat/km.lam.pdf

Libicki, Martin C., Lillian Ablon, and Tim Webb, *Defender's Dilemma: Charting a Course Toward Cybersecurity*, Santa Monica, Calif.: RAND Corporation, RR-1024-JNI, 2015. As of January 30, 2017:
http://www.rand.org/pubs/research_reports/RR1024.html

linfo, "Kernel Definition," undated. As of January 31, 2017:
http://www.linfo.org/kernel.html

Maillart, Thomas, Mingyi Zhao, Jens Grossklags, and John Chuang, "Given Enough Eyeballs, All Bugs Are Shallow? Revisiting Eric Raymond with Bug Bounty Program," University of California, Berkeley, 2016. As of January 30, 2017:
http://weis2016.econinfosec.org/wp-content/uploads/sites/2/2015/08/WEIS_2016_paper_76.pdf

McConnell, Steve, *Code Complete: A Practical Handbook of Software Construction*, 2nd edition, Redmond, Wash.: Microsoft Press, 2004.

Microsoft, "Security Development Lifecycle: Life in the Digital Crosshairs," no date. As of January 30, 2017:
https://www.microsoft.com/security/sdl/story/

———, *Microsoft Security Bulletin*, 1997–2016.

———, *Microsoft Security Intelligence Report (MSIR)*, Vol. 15, January–June 2013. As of January 30, 2017:
http://download.microsoft.com/download/5/0/3/50310CCE-8AF5-4FB4-83E2-03F1DA92F33C/Microsoft_Security_Intelligence_Report_Volume_15_English.pdf

Microsoft Tech Center, "Bounty Hunters: The Honor Roll," 2016a. As of January 30, 2017:
https://technet.microsoft.com/en-us/security/dn469163

———, "Microsoft Bounty Programs," 2016b. As of January 30, 2017:
https://technet.microsoft.com/en-us/security/dn425036

Miller, Charlie, *The Legitimate Vulnerability Market: Inside the Secretive World of 0-Day Exploit Sales*, Independent Security Evaluators, May 6, 2007. As of January 30, 2017:
http://weis2007.econinfosec.org/papers/29.pdf

MITRE, "Common Vulnerabilities and Exposures," undated. As of January 31, 2017:
https://cve.mitre.org/about/

Moore, Tyler, Allan Friedman, and Ariel D. Procaccia, "Would a 'Cyber Warrior' Protect Us: Exploring Trade-Offs Between Attack and Defense of Information Systems," in *Proceedings of the 2010 Workshop on New Security Paradigms*, New York: ACM, 2010, pp. 85–94.

Moussouris, Katie, and Michael Siegel, *The Wolves of Vuln Street: The 1st System Dynamics Model of the 0day Market*, presentation given at RSA Conference 2015, San Francisco, April 20–24, 2015. As of January 30, 2017:
https://www.rsaconference.com/writable/presentations/file_upload/ht-t08-the-wolves-of-vuln-street-the-1st-dynamic-systems-model-of-the-0day-market_final.pdf

Naraine, Ryan, "Stuxnet Attackers Used 4 Windows Zero-Day Exploits," ZDNet, September 14, 2010. As of January 30, 2017:
http://www.zdnet.com/article/stuxnet-attackers-used-4-windows-zero-day-exploits/

National Research Council, *Trust in Cyberspace*, Fred B. Schneider, ed., Washington, D.C.: The National Academies Press, 1999.

———, *Technology, Policy, Law, and Ethics Regarding U.S. Acquisition and Use of Cyberattack Capabilities*, William A. Owens, Kenneth W. Dam, Herbert S. Lin, eds., Washington, D.C.: The National Academies Press, 2009.

National Vulnerability Database, no date. As of February 1, 2017:
http://nvd.nist.gov/

Newsome, James, and Dawn Song, "Dynamic Taint Analysis for Automatic Detection, Analysis, and Signature Generation of Exploits on Commodity Software," Carnegie Mellon University, School of Computer Science, July 2005. As of January 30, 2017:
http://bitblaze.cs.berkeley.edu/papers/taintcheck-full.pdf

No Starch Press, "Security," web page, 2016. As of January 30, 2017:
https://www.nostarch.com/catalog/security

NRC—*See* National Research Council.

Open Web Application Security Project, "Buffer Overflow," undated-a. As of January 21, 2017:
https://www.owasp.org/index.php/Buffer_Overflow

———, "Denial of Service," undated-b. As of January 31, 2017:
https://www.owasp.org/index.php/Denial_of_Service

OWASP—*See* Open Web Application Security Project.

Ozment, Andy, and Stuart E. Schechter, "Milk or Wine: Does Software Security Improve with Age?" paper presented at the 15th USENIX Security Symposium, August 3, 2006. As of January 30, 2017:
https://www.usenix.org/legacy/event/sec06/tech/ozment.html

Pagliery, Jose, "You Make $70k but Cost Your Boss $88k," CNN Money, February 28, 2013. As of January 30, 2017:
http://money.cnn.com/2013/02/28/smallbusiness/salary-benefits/

Ransbotham, S., and S. Mitra, "The Impact of Immediate Disclosure on Attack Diffusion and Volume," in 10th Workshop on Economics of Information Security (WEIS 2011), Fairfax, Va., June 14–15, 2011.

Rescorla, Eric, "Is Finding Security Holes a Good Idea?" *IEEE Security & Privacy*, Vol. 3, No. 1, January–February 2005, pp. 14–19.

Risk-Based Security, "VulnDB—Vulnerability Intelligence," 2017. As of January 30, 2017:
https://www.riskbasedsecurity.com/vulndb/

Salary.com, "Benefits Wizard," 2016, As of January 30, 2017:
http://swz.salary.com/MyBenefits/LayoutScripts/Mbfl_Start.aspx

Schneier, Bruce, "Should U.S. Hackers Fix Cybersecurity Holes or Exploit Them?" *The Atlantic*, May 19, 2014. As of January 30, 2017:
http://www.theatlantic.com/technology/archive/2014/05/should-hackers-fix-cybersecurity-holes-or-exploit-them/371197/

Schryen, Guido, and Eliot Rich, "Increasing Software Security Through Open Source or Closed Source Development? Empirics Suggest That We Have Asked the Wrong Question," paper presented at the 43rd Hawaii International Conference on System Sciences (HICSS), January 5–8, 2010.

Schwartz, Ari, and Rob Knake, "Government's Role in Vulnerability Disclosure: Creating a Permanent and Accountable Vulnerability Equities Process." Discussion Paper 2016-04, Cyber Security Project, Belfer Center for Science and International Affairs, Harvard Kennedy School, June 2016. As of January 30, 2017:
http://belfercenter.ksg.harvard.edu/files/vulnerability-disclosure-web-final3.pdf

Shieber, Jonathan, "Synack Raises $7.5 Million Putting Bounties on IT Security Threats," *Tech Crunch*, April 14, 2014: As of January 30, 2017
https://techcrunch.com/2014/04/24/synack-raises-7-5-million-putting-bounties-on-it-security-threats/

Shryock, Henry S., Jacob S. Siegel, and Elizabeth A. Larmon, *The Methods and Materials of Demography*, Washington, D.C.: U.S. Bureau of the Census, 1973. As of January 30, 2017:
http://demographybook.weebly.com/uploads/2/7/2/5/27251849/david_a._swanson_jacob_s._siegel_the_methods_and_materials_of_demography_second_edition__2004.pdf

StalkR, "Exec Race Condition Exploitations," StalkR's Blog, November 6, 2010. As of January 30, 2017:
http://blog.stalkr.net/2010/11/exec-race-condition-exploitations.html

Techopedia, Bug Bounty, web page, undated-a. As of January 31, 2017:
http://www.techopedia.com/definition/28637/bug-bounty

Techtarget, "heap," undated-a. As of January 31, 2017:
http://whatis.techtarget.com/definition/heap

————, "stack," undated-a. As of January 31, 2017:
http://whatis.techtarget.com/definition/stack

Tsyrklevich, Vlad, "Hacking Team: A Zero-Day Market Case Study," July 22, 2015. As of
January 30, 2017:
https://tsyrklevich.net/2015/07/22/hacking-team-0day-market/

U.S. Office of Personnel Management, "Pay & Leave—Pay Administration," 2016. As of January 30,
2017:
https://www.opm.gov/policy-data-oversight/pay-leave/pay-administration/fact-sheets/
computing-hourly-rates-of-pay-using-the-2087-hour-divisor/

Wikipedia, "Arbitrary Code Execution," undated-a. As of January 31, 2017:
https://en.wikipedia.org/wiki/Arbitrary_code_execution

Zerodium, "Zerodium Payout Ranges," January 2016. As of January 30, 2017:
https://zerodium.com/images/zerodium_prices.png

Zetter, Kim, "When Security Experts Gather to Talk Consensus, Chaos Ensues," *Wired*, October 1,
2015. As of January 30, 2017:
https://www.wired.com/2015/10/security-experts-gather-talk-consensus-chaos-ensues/

Zhao, Mingyi, Jens Grossklags, and Peng Liu, "An Empirical Study of Web Vulnerability Discovery
Ecosystems," in *Proceedings of the 22nd ACM SIGSAC Conference on Computer and Communications
Security*, New York: ACM, 2015.

Zorabedian, John, "How a Hacking Team Got Hacked," *Naked Security*, April 2016. As of
January 30, 2017:
https://nakedsecurity.sophos.com/2016/04/19/how-hacking-team-got-hacked/